This Hemisphere of Liberty
A Philosophy of the Americas

Michael Novak

PACKBACK EDITION

With a new preface by the author

The AEI Press

Publisher for the American Enterprise Institute
WASHINGTON, D.C.

1992

All but one of the chapters in this book were first prepared as lectures to be given in Latin America, and several have already been published there in translation (especially in Estudios Publicos *of Santiago,Chile). The versions printed here have been significantly revised and nearly all appear in English for the first time. I am grateful to the Institute for Contemporary Studies (San Francisco, California) for allowing me to include chapter 7, "Wealth and Virtue," which, in another version, was presented at an ICS conference in 1989. I owe thanks as well to the Bradley Foundation for the lectureship under which the appendix on St. Thomas Aquinas was presented. Finally, I owe thanks to David Foster, who saw the original manuscript through the long editorial process and to Kevin O'Halloran, who helped in the very last stages of the proofs.*

To order call toll free 1-800-462-6420 or 1-717-794-3800. For all other inquiries please contact the AEI Press, 1150 Seventeenth Street, N.W., Washington, D.C. 20036 or call 1-800-862-5801.

Library of Congress Cataloging-in-Publication Data

Novak, Michael.

    This hemisphere of liberty: a philosophy of the Americas / Michael Novak.
      p. cm. —
    Includes index.
    ISBN 0-8447-3735-6
    ISBN 978 0-8447-3736-2, paperback edition
    1. Liberty. 2. Social ethics. 3. Latin America—Economic conditions—1982– 4. Latin America—Politics and government—1980–
    5. Free enterprise—Latin America. 6. Church and social problems—Latin America. I. Title. II. Series.
    JC599.L3N68 1990
    323.44'098—dc20   90-37328
                                          CIP

To those—in Mexico, Chile, Brazil, Argentina, Peru, Colombia, Venezuela, Panama, El Salvador, Guatemala, Costa Rica, and the Dominican Republic—who have invited me to lecture in Latin America and directed my eyes toward our common destiny.

Contents

Preface to the Paperback Edition

Since *This Hemisphere of Liberty* first appeared, several Latin American economies have moved in new and creative directions, most notably (following the example of Chile) Mexico and Argentina; the results have been dramatic, as *The Economist* noted in its cover story of April 18–24, 1992, "Latin America Cheers Up."[1]

The fall of socialism during 1989–1991 helped to generate a new climate of liberty in Latin America. Former Socialists have quietly been discarding outmoded economic thinking; party buttons have been falling like leaves. With its total dependence on subsidies from the former USSR nakedly revealed, the economic condition of Cuba has torn away the illusions of many. For others, the successes of Chile and Mexico have inspired new hopes.

More and more people seem to be recognizing that the greatest single resource of Latin America is its own people. Economies work better when human persons are given institutional support to become creators of wealth, not merely dependents on government. Slowly the perception is growing: development works best "from the bottom up." Development means empowering the poor to incorporate their own businesses, to own their own land, to improve their education and skills, and to exercise their God-given right to personal economic initiative. Thus, governments must change laws so that the poor can freely enter markets, obtain credit for new small businesses, and establish such businesses legally, cheaply, and quickly. Such is the road to people's capitalism—"barefoot capitalism," as Guy Sorman calls it.

This revolution has a long way to go, of course. In most of Latin America, many laws still repress the economic activism of the poor. The poor are effectively prevented from engaging in business except illegally. Such laws must be changed.

The international agencies, too, need to reorient their own strategic thinking away from helping governments and established elites, toward encouraging and supporting small businesses. (Out of 197 developmental projects in Brazil in recent years, for example, the World Bank funded only 2 in the private sector.) For the future of this hemisphere lies with the promotion of millions of new small businesses, especially among the poor, who have so far been excluded from economic growth. Unless capitalism is inclusive and universal, it is not really capitalism at all; it is only another form of patrimonialism, directed and limited by state power.

The stunning encyclical of Pope John Paul II, *Centesimus Annus* (May 2, 1991) has also raised spirits. Besieged by questions from all over the world about what form of political economy he would recommend to third world nations, the Holy Father called attention to the collapse of socialism. Without in any way wishing to justify triumphalism on the part of capitalism, or to commit the Catholic church to any one worldly system, the pope nonetheless spoke affirmatively of "an economic system which recognizes the fundamental and positive role of business, the market, private property . . . as well as free human creativity in the economic sector" (*Centesimus Annus*, no. 42). He rejected a "radical capitalist ideology" that does not circumscribe business activities by a "strong juridical framework" and "ethical and religious" norms. He called the attention of business leaders, in effect, to "the moral, cultural and political responsibilities of business" (see chapter 8 in this volume).

But paragraph 32 of that encyclical is especially germane to this book (see chapter 4), and I wish to reproduce parts of it here. After writing about the land as the traditional form of wealth, the pope turns to the human mind as a cause of wealth—the human mind exercised in science, discovery, technical skill, and enterprise—and points out its corporate and personal dimensions:

> In our time, in particular, there exists another form of ownership which is becoming no less important than land: *the possession of know-how, technology and skill.* The wealth of the industrialized nations is based much more on this kind of ownership than on natural resources.
>
> Mention has just been made of the fact that *people work with each other*, sharing in a "community of work" which embraces ever widening circles. A person who produces something other than for his own use generally does so in order that others may use it after they have paid a just price, mutually agreed upon through free bargaining. It is precisely the ability to foresee both the needs of others and the combinations of productive factors most adapted to satisfying those needs that constitutes another important source of wealth in modern society. Besides, many goods cannot be adequately produced through the work of an isolated individual; they require the cooperation of many people in working towards a common goal. Organizing such a produc-

tive effort, planning its duration in time, making sure that it corresponds in a positive way to the demands which it must satisfy, and taking the necessary risks—all this too is a source of wealth in today's society. In this way, the *role* of disciplined and creative *human work* and, as an essential part of that work, *initiative and entrepreneurial ability* becomes increasingly evident and decisive.

This process, which throws practical light on a truth about the person which Christianity has constantly affirmed, should be viewed carefully and favourably. Indeed, besides the earth, man's principal resource is *man himself*. His intelligence enables him to discover the earth's productive potential and the many different ways in which human needs can be satisfied. It is his disciplined work in close collaboration with others that makes possible the creation of ever more extensive *working communities* which can be relied upon to transform man's natural and human environments. Important virtues are involved in this process, such as diligence, industriousness, prudence in undertaking reasonable risks, reliability and fidelity in interpersonal relationships, as well as courage in carrying out decisions which are difficult and painful but necessary, both for the overall working of a business and in meeting possible setbacks [*Centesimus Annus*, no. 32].

Even when Pope John Paul II calls for profound changes in the structure of the world economy, the direction in which these changes point is plain to see: not only to pursue the objectives stated in *Rerum Novarum* (1891), including "a sufficient wage for the support of a family, social insurance for old age and unemployment, and adequate protection for the conditions of employment"; and "to lighten, defer or even cancel the debt" of third world countries where payment, although just, would lead to "unbearable sacrifices"; but also to look upon the poor as creators, made in the image of God, with respect for their right to personal economic initiative; to include them in the international circle of education, training, and the development of human skills; to include them in "fair access to the international market," with respect for "the proper use of [their own] human resources"; "to help these needy people to acquire expertise, to enter the circle of exchange, and to develop their skills in order to make the best use of their capacities and resources" (see nos. 33–35).

And again:

It is necessary to break down the barriers and monopolies which leave so many countries on the margins of development, and to provide all individuals and nations with the basic conditions which will enable them to share in development. This goal calls for programmed and responsible efforts on the part of the entire international community.

The pope here assigns separate but linked responsibilities to the stronger and the weaker nations:

> Stronger nations must offer weaker ones opportunities for taking their place in international life, and the latter must learn how to use these opportunities by making the necessary efforts and sacrifices and by ensuring political and economic stability, the certainty of better prospects for the future, the improvement of workers' skills, and the training of competent business leaders who are conscious of their responsibilities [no. 35].

These words of the pope leave all of us, both in the advanced and in the less-developed countries, with much to do. They fall squarely in what I have called in the appendix "the Catholic Whig tradition." Indeed, my own suggestions for an international program that meets the criteria of Pope John Paul II are contained here in chapters 6 and 9 (pp. 55–56 and 105–6).

The warm welcome afforded this book in Latin America has given me hope that efforts to supply a framework for understanding are useful. Encouragement for the project of a "Catholic Whig tradition" has been especially satisfying. My thanks, once again, to my friends in Latin America.

MICHAEL NOVAK

---

1. See also "Latin America: The Big Move to Free Markets," *Business Week*, June 15, 1992.

1
Introduction—Building Bridges

Experience teaches that unless one understands the Catholic intellectual traditions of southern Europe and Latin America, one cannot really enter the horizon of Latin American intellectual discourse. Many Latin Americans do not think of themselves as Catholic at all, and many may be quite irreligious. But even the irreligious have become used to expressing themselves within the horizon of Latin Catholic history.

For that reason, more than most writers about the Americas, in this book I sometimes use an explicitly Catholic language even in talking about political economy. Strictly, it would not have been necessary to do so; the same points might have been just as well expressed in secular categories—and these would be more familiar to North Americans. But that choice would have prevented many important readers in Latin America from understanding—even more, might have led to misunderstanding—since many bishops, theologians, religious, and lay activists often understand best when historical religious language is employed.

Moreover, I have encountered in my travels many writers and scholars in Latin America who, while not Catholic, find the language of northern Anglo-American political economy too emotionally and culturally thin, too materialistic in its timbre, too individualistic in its intonation, too drily pragmatic. For many in Latin America, the smell of incense at the High Mass, the flickering candles and their smoke, the bells, the sonorous hymns, and the taste of the Lord's Body on the tongue convey a sensibility that is far thicker than that received in the bare white Puritan churches of New England (just as Nathaniel Hawthorne in *The Marble Faun* struggled under an analogous cultural contrast between Boston and Rome).

A highly cultured people, furthermore, necessarily carries with it a profoundly conservative sensibility. Painfully aware of the richness and complexity of the past, they revel in holding onto that past and recreating it. Partly, they live in memory as birds in air. Their imaginations need the past as certain fauna live only in the tangled jungle; one sees this vividly in Latin American novelists. Thus, nearly all Latin Americans, even the most radical, nourish a conservative consciousness, sometimes under the banner of "national identity." They identify themselves with past events, heroes, movements, struggles. Progressives in Latin America are seldom purely progressive; most want to carry their past proudly with them as they advance.

Is this in itself a Catholic inclination? A church fashioned around the eucharistic instruction, "Do this in memory of Me," inclines the appetites of the soul toward memory. A church that delights in a sensuous liturgy inclines the soul toward a thickly textured imagination, by contrast with which the more Protestant culture of North America seems to be plain, direct, and disappointingly literal.

For such reasons, Anglo-American terms for various tendencies in political economy echo quite oddly in Latin America. Such terms as "conservative" or "liberal," "radical" or "reactionary," "progressive" and "traditionalist" have a quite different resonance in the two continents of this hemisphere. And the one intellectual tradition, in particular, that I want to tap and to articulate in this book cannot be expressed in such terms. This tradition borrows a little from each of these other tendencies, conservative and progressive and the rest. Some years ago, for example, the great Polish philosopher Leszek Kolakowski described himself as a "conservative progressive liberal socialist," and it occurred to me later that this description plausibly reflects the complex reality of most Catholic cultures in the modern world.

Catholic horizons go back farther than those of modernity. These horizons include, in the smoky background of the past, a dark and blazing web of popes, saints, villains, and heroes stretching back for centuries. They also include a strong sense of the coming kingdom of God up ahead in the future—the very image that Marx borrowed for his proletarian paradise. They include a love for clear logic and also for a dark and tortured psychology. They include a rich love for the liberal arts, painting, music, and dance and rather less love for cold science and mathematics. "Conservative-progressive," indeed.

To call attention, therefore, to the unique and distinctive complex of mental tendencies that speaks to the Latin American condition (and to my own), I have coined for this book the phrase "the Catholic Whig tradition." Actually, I owe the first suggestions for this concept to Friedrich von Hayek, who reminded me in his famous postscript to *The Constitution of Liberty*, "Why I Am Not a Conservative," that Lord Acton had called Thomas Aquinas the first Whig. Hayek noted that no one who favors, as Hayek does, such dynamic principles as a free economy (and democracy and pluralism) can be described fairly as a conservative. The proper name for such a person would be progressive, but that name has been captured by Socialists, who want to reduce all economics and morals to politics, a politics, at that, firmly in the hands of the central state. Not being a conservative or a progressive, then, Hayek betook himself to Lord Acton's suggestion and called himself a Whig, explicitly citing Aquinas as a useful model. I myself have found this very helpful. (The appendix to this book follows up Lord Acton's suggestion about Aquinas in detail, and incidentally clarifies the ancient Whig pedigree, far older than the now defunct British and American parties of that name.) Bellarmine, Alexis de Tocqueville, Jacques Maritain, Yves R. Simon, and others discussed later may also be counted in this tradition.

In some sense, the Catholic Whigs resemble progressives. They believe in the dignity of the human person, in human liberty, in institutional reform, in gradual progress. But they also have a deep respect for language, law, liturgy, custom, habit, and tradition that marks them, simultaneously, as conservatives. With the conservatives, the Catholic Whigs have an awareness of the force of cultural habit and the role of passion and sin in human affairs. With the liberals, they give central importance to human liberty, especially the slow building of institutions of liberty.

The Catholic Whigs see liberty as *ordered* liberty—not the liberty to do what one wishes, but the liberty to do what one ought—much as Thomas Aquinas saw practical wisdom as ordered reason, *recta ratio.* Often embattled by the Church's traditionalists and fundamentalists, the Catholic Whigs have championed the value of progress in history, progress above all along the axis of liberty; but their progressive instincts are tempered by an acute sense of irony, tragedy, and contingency. They prefer to stress steady institutional progress, achieved gradually and solidly, and well rooted in cultural habit. They distrust merely abstract principles and spasms of revolutionary fervor.

Undoubtedly, the best way to convey the essence of the Catholic Whig tradition is to show it at work, rather than to attempt to define it in thin abstract terms. This tradition represents a point of view, a set of expectations about human action and the course of history, and an inner drive to enlarge the dimension of conscience. It wishes to bring human life increasingly under the gentle sway of human reflection and choice, rather than of passion, bigotry, prejudice, or material interest. The Statue of Liberty is a good symbol of its inmost disposition: a lamp of reason held up against the fog, a book of the laws held over the heart; a beacon for the future, firmly implanted on the wisdom of the past.

Each of the following chapters aims to bring this tradition into clearer focus. Still, this intellectual tradition is only the horizon within which we are working; it should not distract our gaze from the substance of the matter. Our true subject is how to build institutions of liberty in this hemisphere of the Americas, this original home of liberty, from which liberty (as Tocqueville noted) has rippled outward to every quarter of the world, to Europe first of all, and in our day even into the Soviet Union, China, and Africa. This hemisphere of the Americas has been the crucible of the world's liberty, the birthplace of modern institutions of liberty—of religious pluralism, of constitutional democracy, and of the free and dynamic economy of development. The Old World taught the New World much, but the New World taught the Old World liberty. From here were kindled the first fires that now blaze up around the entire planet.

It is true that there remains much to do in this hemisphere. Millions upon millions live in destitution, a state even below that of poverty. Scores of millions remain unemployed, despite the immense amount of work that needs to be done, and many millions more are underemployed. Even more, a majority of Latin America's poor are barred from incorporating their own small businesses or qualifying for credit (the mother's milk of small businesses), and are obliged to work as "illegals" or "informals." In the precapitalist mode, Latin American economies are characterized by markets, private property, and profits. These do not, contrary to Marx, suffice to constitute a capitalist system. Latin America offers few legal or cultural supports for the essential mark of the capitalist economy: enterprise, innovation, creativity. Its traditional system of (insecure) property ownership is limited to the few, as are the opportunities it offers to economic activism. Thus, even when people work very hard (for very little recompense), there is surprisingly little economic activism; there is, in places, a kind of torpor that comes from defeat and lack of opportunity. In a word, the full liberation of Latin America, especially its economic liberation, has not yet been accomplished.

The present book grows out of many trips to Latin America during the turbulent years of the 1980s. I had been asked to lecture in Brazil, Argentina, Chile, Colombia, Peru, Guatemala, El Salvador, Panama, and Mexico. Indeed, earlier versions of the chapters that follow were developed from these occasions. They have been revised in the light of the many animated discussions and newspaper articles that ensued.

Those who invited me usually asked me to adapt the arguments I had begun to make in *The Spirit of Democratic Capitalism* (1982) and *Will It Liberate? Questions about Liberation Theology (1986)*, both of which have appeared in Spanish and Portuguese. They asked me to meet further questions that arose specifically from Latin American circumstances. These seminars and discussions taught me a great deal and forced me to think about many matters I had not confronted before. They carried me into areas and toward insights that I had not earlier explored. Attentive readers will, therefore, find much here that is new. Many fresh empirical materials had to be confronted; new difficulties solved; new arguments formulated.

In particular, I was driven to think much harder about the role of human discovery and creativity in dynamic, developing systems; about the specific nature of the moral and intellectual virtue of enterprise; about the close tie between the Catholic Whig concept of the person and its correlative concept of community; about differences between Latin and Anglo-American intellectual traditions; about the ways in which the unguarded use of common words (such as "capitalism," "markets," "enterprise," "liberty," "individualism," "family," and many others) often result in intercultural misunderstanding. Experience warns me that I have probably not yet succeeded in translating my own way of thinking into words fully meaningful in Latin American discourse. Much more, doubtless, needs to be done. But the only way I know to achieve this is through public and civil exchange of criticism and comment. Many disagreements turn out on inspection to be mutual misunderstandings. Much patience and many hours of discussion are needed to get to the point at which all parties see truly and exactly where they agree and disagree—and why. To reach real disagreement is a very high art.

The text that follows is predominantly philosophical. It belongs to the branch of *practical* philosophy, however, since its intention is to direct doing and making, not solely to display the good definitions and clear logic of a speculative system. To men and women of action, practical philosophy is highly useful; more mistakes are made through intellectual inadvertence than the unreflective activist, always in a hurry, may care to note. And small mistakes made at the beginning of an enterprise often grow into giants by journey's end— which can mean, and in our century has often meant, ruin. I belong, therefore, to that school of activists who believe that sound reflection is of great assistance in large practical undertakings and that a realistic and historically informed point of view is likely to save activists from many self-destructive errors.

The first chapter takes up the first practical philosophical theme, ordered liberty. The second examines the priority of community inherent in the constitution of the free person—and the priority of the free person inherent in the constitution of the free society. This

5

mutual codefinition of person and community is a foundational concept, without which the democratic republic and the capitalist economy become unbalanced.

In the third chapter, I stress two related points. The first is the primacy of morals over politics and economics. Only from the dynamic energy of moral striving (including ideas and habits, as well as institutions embodying them) can a political economy take life. The second is the economic creativity that makes a democratic republic work. The primacy of morals must be maintained if the societies now being formed are to serve the cause of liberty. And for those made in the image of their Creator, creativity is the dynamic principle of morals, a this-worldly expression of love—even of what Dante called "the Love that moves the sun and all the stars."

After that, there follow practical chapters on institutional structures, ethics, and the moral arguments for capitalism that Scottish Whigs advanced before capitalism came to be.

My aim is to present a philosophical horizon open to realists who seek liberty. It is also to build bridges between those who think in Latin and Catholic terms and those whose cultural context is rather more Anglo-Saxon and Protestant.[1] This is a large task. I can hope barely to have begun it.

My overriding conviction is that the Creator has tied our continents together, North and South, and instilled in us a profound passion for liberty. We have not yet achieved the full liberation of our peoples, especially the poor—liberty from torture and tyranny through constitutional republics, liberty from poverty through free and dynamic economies, and liberty from all oppression of information, ideas, and conscience.

Liberty is the true destiny of this hemisphere and, through it, of the world.

2
Reconstituting
a Social Order

In every quarter of the world, citizens can hear the branches of dead political ideas come crashing to the ground. Everywhere systems are undergoing transformation. In these times, the truth of Pascal's *pensée* penetrates the heart: "The first moral obligation is to think clearly."

This is especially true in reconstituting a social order. In such a task, mistakes about the human person, community, or the causes of wealth can have consequences fateful for a hundred years. To think socially, these days, is to think not only for the present generation.

The Return to "Ordered Liberty"

Through the next three chapters, I want to summon up the distinctive and proven strength of what I call the Catholic Whig tradition as a useful philosophy for Latin America, Eastern Europe, and elsewhere. The advantage of this tradition is that its animating drive is to see reality true. Its most highly prized virtue is practical wisdom. Its four basic concepts are "ordered liberty," the person, the community, and creativity. Its sources—if not its name—go back to the Book of Genesis, Aristotle, and St. Thomas Aquinas. Its most original institutional successes have appeared in this hemisphere—the hemisphere of liberty.

In turning to this tradition at this time, we in the Americas are not alone. A leader of the opposition movement in Hungary, G. M. Tamas, declared in 1988 that the political future of Eastern Europe depends upon a renewal of the Whig tradition. Tamas recognized that the traditionalists of Eastern Europe long ago betrayed truth and liberty. They clung to tradition because it was tradition, not because it was true. Tradition lost its legitimacy. In rejecting communism, Eastern Europe must turn to a tradition of liberty but not just to *any* tradition of liberty:

> Western-style Whiggish neo-conservatism is now being created in Poland and Hungary. It has to be Whiggish . . . we

7

have to reject some of our own traditions which contradict it. . . . But we will appear to be and will be to a certain extent, liberals.

Tamas is quite clear about what he means by this:

Neo-conservatives, New Old Whigs, or whatever they are labelled . . . try to re-establish the authority of the legitimate constitutional state and the unencumbered freedom of the market—both based on choice, that is, free will and on the ensuing responsibility which attaches to choice.

Only a form of "ordered liberty" will suffice. The task will not be easy. Tamas warns that

we will have to sail uncharted seas. No one has ever seen a post-communist society. We will be the first generation to see it (perhaps, like Moses, only from afar) and we will have to borrow legitimacy from the Western canon.[1]

In brief, Eastern Europeans, as well as many others, are clearly returning to the Whig tradition of ordered liberty.

What Is the Catholic Whig Tradition?

Thomas Jefferson once wrote of North America that, with respect to rights, "there was but one opinion on this side of the water. All American Whigs thought alike on these subjects."[2] By Whigs he meant "The Party of Liberty" at the time of the American Revolution; believers in republican government or government by the people; and those intent upon creating, in accord with nature and nature's God, a "system of natural liberty." I also want to highlight a stream of Catholic thought of similar inspiration. I call it the Catholic Whig tradition, but to my knowledge, no one has ever called the *philosophia perennis* by this exact name before (although Walter Lippmann in *The Public Philosophy* came close). The existence of the tradition is, however, plain enough. It is also plain that the Whig tradition—and in particular the Catholic Whig tradition—is beginning to enjoy an intellectual renaissance. It has become the alternative both to traditionalism and to progressivism, both to the Left and to the Right.

It is characteristic of the Whig tradition to teach by pointing to examples, to personal embodiments, rather than solely to theories. In that spirit, let me point to John Paul II as the pontiff who most deserves the name of Catholic Whig. Among the principles central to his social thought are: creativity, liberty, solidarity, and anti-utopian realism. He has called religious liberty the first and most fundamental human right. His many speeches on religious liberty show him to be

8

as passionate a defender of liberty of conscience as Thomas Jefferson. He defines his favorite concept, "solidarity," in terms of freedom of conscience.[3] He has issued through Joseph, Cardinal Ratzinger two long letters on Christian liberation and Christian liberty. In *Sollicitudo Rei Socialis* he has linked the right to religious liberty to the right to personal economic enterprise. And this right, he says, flows directly from the creative subjectivity of the human person, made in the image of the Creator. Pope John Paul II asks human beings today to contribute new chapters to the history of liberty. In Chile and elsewhere, he has said that democratic institutions and democratic habits are the sole worldly guarantors of human rights.[4]

Yet even before Pope John Paul II, the Catholic Whig tradition had a long history. Thus, as Friedrich von Hayek notes, Lord Acton was not being altogether paradoxical when he called St. Thomas Aquinas "the first Whig."[5] By that designation, Lord Acton intended to emphasize the importance of St. Thomas in the history of liberty. Among others who may be counted as model figures in this long history are Robert Bellarmine, Richard Hooker, the Jesuits of Salamanca, Alexis de Tocqueville, and Lord Acton. Among recent exponents have been Don Luigi Sturzo, Jacques Maritain, Yves R. Simon, John Courtney Murray, S. J., Hayek's countryman Wilhelm Roepke, Chancellor Konrad Adenauer and his economic minister, Ludwig Erhard.

All such thinkers manifested a *social* vision. They were concerned with the shape that whole societies should assume, to do justice to the moral personality of human persons. All had a sharp sense of the contingencies, ironies, and tragedies of human history. They saw probabilities (but not certainties) of human social progress. They respected the durability of existing habits, customs, laws, and traditions; but this respect did not prevent them from thinking of newer and better levels of achievement. The Catholic Whigs had unusually clear ideas about the dignity of the human person and the inviolable depths of human conscience. But they also emphasized the primacy of community, and they meant by community not a mere collective, not a kinship network, not a tribal or ethnic or national whole, and certainly not a herd or hive. They meant a community of free persons.

When the Whigs define themselves as the Party of Liberty, furthermore, they define liberty in a special way. They do not mean libertinism or any other disordered form of liberty, such as a supposed "liberty to do whatever one feels like doing." For them, a liberty undirected by reflection and choice is slavery. For them, liberty must be achieved through a self-mastery that nourishes reflection and choice. Such self-mastery is won by slowly gaining dominion

9

over appetite, passion, ignorance, and whim. For them, the enabling agent and protector of liberty is virtue—indeed, a full quiver of virtues, one against each of the vices that commonly deprive human persons of their liberty. In every age, there are many ways in which persons may suffer from a disordered loss of liberty. In our day, drug addiction, alcoholism, and even "temporary insanity" are widely seen to deprive normal persons of their liberty. But so do passion, ignorance, and whim. For the North American founders, therefore, it sufficed to sing in the old hymn:

> Confirm thy soul in self-control
> Thy liberty in law.

Again, the Statue of Liberty in New York harbor stands as a symbol of the Whig conception of liberty. It is a lady, not a warrior—Lady Philosophy, Wisdom. Sober and dignified is the Whig model of liberty: the virtuous woman, the virtuous man. In Miami, in 1987, Pope John Paul II referred to this conception, common to America and to the Whigs, as "ordered liberty."[6] Exactly right. Its sources lie in Genesis, Aristotle, and Cicero: in Jerusalem, Athens, and Rome.

It is also characteristic of the Catholic Whigs to reject abstract utopias, rationalism, and what Pascal referred to as geometric thinking. Instead, they emphasize the crucial role of practical intellect, which Aristotle called practical wisdom and in the Middle Ages was called prudence. These are concepts closely related to the choice of Providence as a favorite name of God, described at great length by St. Thomas Aquinas in the third book of the *Summa contra Gentiles*. For Whigs it makes a great difference that God should be conceived of as concerned with singulars, contingents, and individual agents who are free, rather than as a Geometer God, interested solely in necessities, general commands, logic, and irresistible laws.

The Whig Alternative

As even this brief survey suggests, the Catholic Whigs share with all other progressives a certain hope in the capacities of human beings for approaching ever more closely "the building up in history of the kingdom of God." They share with traditionalists a sharp sense of limits and a sense of sin. They believe that by God's grace and promises, through a fuller exercise of charity and practical intellect, human beings can make steady progress in arriving at more just societies, but also that, through sin, such progress is reversible and may descend even to the gates of hell—as in our century it has.

In a balanced way, the Whigs value deeply all that the human race has learned and embodied, often in tacit ways, in existing habits, institutions, and traditions. They do not think that their grandparents were less wise than they. They spend much effort learning from the past, trying to put into words its often tacit wisdom. They think of themselves as part of a living tradition and therefore are as much oriented toward the future as they are respectful of the past. They are wary of ideology, which they regard as a form of rationalism untutored by experience.[7] They are not afraid to dream, and yet they have a special regard for things tried, tested, and found to be true. They think it foolish not to learn from the hard-won lessons of the past and foolish, too, to ignore the new needs of the human pilgrimage barely discernible in the near future.

In this respect, the classic Whig vision is rooted in the cautious optimism that springs from reflection on human experience in the light of original sin. Their caution makes Whigs seem to utopians too pessimistic. Their optimism makes them seem to traditionalists too visionary. Nonetheless, the Whig vision represents rather well the wisdom of Judaism, Christianity, and the best among the Greeks and Romans concerning human nature and human sin. Whigs hold that every human being sometimes sins. Therefore, they conclude, no man should be trusted with total power. They hold simultaneously that most people most of the time (but not always) act with generosity, decency, compassion, and creativity. The first of these beliefs makes checks and balances necessary. The second makes realistic human progress possible.

The Commercial Republic

One of the great achievements of the Whig tradition was its new world experiment, the *Novus Ordo Seclorum* (the new order of the ages). Its American progenitors called that experiment the commercial republic.[8] The Whigs were the first philosophers in history to grasp the importance of basing government of the people upon the foundation of commerce. They underpinned democracy with a capitalist, growing economy.

Before the modern Whigs, most philosophers in history had little respect for commerce. For this they had some justification. In premodern, no-growth economies, economic activities were a zero-sum game. Commercial middle-men wrestled for advantage at both ends, with their suppliers and their purchasers—both of whom fought back. Commercial activities under such conditions were often nasty, boorish, and curt. Only when commerce became free, when invention drove demand, did the balance of power in commercial activities shift to the customer. At that point, the manners of commerce decisively changed. When sellers owned basics that customers had to have, sellers could be surly. When they began to sell new goods and services never seen before, customers needed to be persuaded, and sellers needed to become more civil. Sellers had to learn new tones of voice—and "sales pitch" became a synonym for the supplication "Please buy."

By 1776, the reputation of persons of commerce was not much higher than it had been when Christ threw the money changers out of the temple. Adam Smith, in a book of a thousand pages, said scarcely a good word for men of business. "People of the same trade seldom meet together, even for merriment and diversion," he said, "but the conversation ends in a conspiracy against the publick, or in some contrivance to raise prices."[9] But while he did not greatly admire individuals in commerce, Smith had learned from his studies an enormous respect for the institutions of commerce. He found that enterprise is the cause of the wealth of nations and that, better than state-directed markets, free markets serve the common good. Competition is nature's own protection against the wounds that original sin implants in every ego; through it, ambition is made to counteract ambition. Political power over the economy breeds closed markets, serves elites, preserves privilege, freezes initiative, and promotes stagnation and decline. Free economies advance the common prosperity and uplift the poor better than statist ones.

Smith pioneered in seeing the benefits that commerce might bring to world development, human interdependence, and international concord. He foresaw a world united by commerce, as neither religion nor military power nor political imperium could unite it. Since it protects business contracts across national lines, a reliable body of international law is in the profoundest interest of commerce. Since it depends on voluntary agreements maintained for long periods, commerce further teaches its participants to be "other-regarding" (if not quite altruistic, at least to show for others due and reciprocal concern). Thus, threads of commerce unite the human race, weave it together, make it a whole many-colored robe.

Thomas Jefferson thought Adam Smith's *Wealth of Nations*, "the best book extant" on political economy.[10] By 1787, most of the framers of the U.S. Constitution who met in Philadelphia had read Adam Smith. And with his help they succeeded in designing "a commercial republic," not quite the first in the world (Venice, Amsterdam, and others had preceded them in some respects), but certainly the first to limit so severely the powers of government over the economy. They empowered economic institutions to act as full equals to political institutions—not *under* them, but beside them and free.

Smith had written of "political economy." For the first time, "polity" and "economy" became independent and yet interdependent and might be pictured as opposite angles at the base of a powerful pyramid, each equally necessary to the soaring up of its peak. Thus, the American framers believed that a democratic polity depends upon a free, dynamic, growing economy and that a growing economy depends upon a free polity.

Only a free economy ensures citizens of financial independence from state control. Only a growing economy defeats envy—that perennial destroyer of civil peace and heedless wrecker of earlier republican experiments. Only a dynamic economy produces the abundance that amply rewards the laborer and causes him to love the republic that makes his labor fruitful. Only in a peaceful republic with a prosperous economy are citizens easily convinced that to contribute to the health of their social system is to serve their own self-interest. Because the early Americans (like many immigrants today) had personally experienced the frustration of their labor in other systems, they recognized a sound and beneficent system as a great boon that yielded vastly greater rewards for the same amount of labor. Such a system seemed to them no enemy. On the contrary, every day they thanked God for it, as Crevecoeur had testified on his visit to America:

> The American ought therefore to love this country much better than that wherein either he or his forefathers were born. Here the rewards of his industry follow with equal steps the progress of his labour; his labour is founded on the basis of nature, *self-interest*; can it want a stronger allurement? Wives and children, who before in vain demanded of him a morsel of bread, now, fat and frolicsome, gladly help their father to clear those fields whence exuberant crops are to arise to feed and to clothe them all; without any part being claimed, either by a despotic prince, a rich abbot, or a mighty lord.[11]

To love such a system was, in a way, to love themselves. To help that system grow, to sacrifice for it, was in their deepest personal interest. In such cases, civic interest and self-interest coincide, as Alexis de Tocqueville described in *Democracy in America*.[12]

The limited state promoting self-government also liberates the free economy, in order that self-government might include the dynamic power of personal initiative, through economic independence from the state. The Whig idea included ordered liberty both in the polity and in the economy. Its aim was to inspire creativity in both and thus to expand the space for all other liberties, civic and moral as well. The distinctive originality of the modern Whigs lay in discerning clearly the liberating role of the humble sphere of commerce—so much disdained by earlier philosophers—and not only the nobler spheres of politics, civic life, and desires of the human spirit. Classical writers, they believed, had turned too early to these nobler spheres and too much neglected such lowly matters as the "merely useful." Upon the stone that earlier builders had rejected they built.

Summary

All around this small planet today, the peoples of the world are turning again to the Whig tradition, to learn how to constitute for themselves systems under which citizens will freely consent to live. They are constituting new nations, or new orders within old nations. The eyes of many are upon things much larger than the self—that is, upon the design or constitution of new social systems. Because they want to protect personal liberties, their thoughts and actions go beyond mere individualism. They try to conceive of practical arrangements within which whole societies will achieve a higher level of the common good than was attainable under earlier arrangements. They think that true community requires an unprecedented respect for individual persons. By following this line of thought, the Whig tradition has gradually introduced into history a new conception of the human person and a new conception of community. These are the philosophical foundations of the modern democratic republic. These are the source of the modern ideal of ordered liberty.

In the slow unfolding of human experience, the Whig tradition discerns and celebrates three liberations (from which the Whig tradition derives its other name, the *liberal* Whig tradition). Whig liberals, through their attention to experience rather than to abstract ideas and through their emphasis upon community as well as upon the individual, are different from utilitarian liberals such as Jeremy Bentham or John Stuart Mill. With such liberals, although on different philosophical grounds, the Whigs promote liberation from torture and tyranny, through political liberty. They promote liberation from poverty, through economic liberty. And they promote liberation from the suppression of conscience, information, and ideas, through the severely limited state.

The social agenda of the Whigs is, therefore, as three-sided as the nature of human beings. Every woman and every man is a political agent, an economic agent, and a seeker after truth, justice, and love. In all three dimensions, the Whigs are the Party of Liberty—more precisely, of Ordered Liberty.

3
Priority of Community, Priority of Persons

One of the fundamental principles of the Catholic Whig tradition is ordered liberty. Another is the codefinition of community and person. A true community respects free persons; an inadequate or false community does not. Correlatively, a fully developed person is capable of knowing and loving; but these are exactly the two human capacities that are inherently communitarian. Note again the codefinition: to be a free person is to know and to love others in community—and a community is true when, in the ordinary circumstances of daily life, its institutions and practices enable persons to multiply the frequency of their acts of knowing and loving. False community represses capacities for reflection and choice. True community enlarges them. These are the lessons that guided the new human experiment in the Americas, in the city aptly named for the love of brothers, Philadelphia.

Community, the Primal Experience of the Americas

The primal experience of the two continents in this hemisphere has been the struggle to build new communities. When Columbus departed from Seville, and when the first pilgrims departed from Leyden, Holland, to set sail across the great Atlantic for what they would call New Spain and New England, they knew what they would *not* find waiting for them. They would not find warm inns with cheerful fires in fireplaces already built. They would not find fields ripe with grain, already protected by soundly built fences. On the contrary, they were pursuing an errand into a wilderness. The work of building up cities and homes loomed in front of them as a formidable task. Nearly everything they were to have they would have to build themselves. Climate and environment might well be more hostile than they could withstand. No one man alone could survive. The future depended on their ability to build communities and to build them in such fashion as would take root and eventually prosper.

While they were very conscious indeed of building a *new* world, and even then were beginning to imagine a *new order,* our ancestors were far from indifferent to tradition. They brought books, ideas, artifacts, tools, and goods that they could not at first hope to make for themselves. Even on shipboard, their faces were turned toward the immense tasks of building cities, churches, civic buildings, markets, and even facilities for woodworks, metal shops, brickyards, ironworks, glassworks, and all the other crafts and trades indispensable for the fairly high levels of common life to which they had been accustomed.

Our ancestors also brought with them a complex heritage of ideas. Some historians of the American experience emphasize the radical break between the ancient, classic tradition of the "liberal" arts and the modern liberal tradition. The first springs from Plato and Aristotle, the second from Hobbes. The first roots itself in natural law, the second in natural rights. The first holds that humans are by nature social animals; the second holds that in "the state of nature" human is to human as wolf to wolf. By its harshness, the second injects a realism and an ardent desire for checks and balances sufficient to make a new experiment more likely to succeed. The first grounds the hope of genuine human progress and success that are proper to the social constitution of the human heart and mind.

The Old and the New

Nevertheless, the conflict between these two visions—that of the ancients and that of the moderns—must not be exaggerated. The formal light under which the ancients looked at nature was different from the formal light under which Hobbes, for example, looked at the state of nature. The ancients noted the ideal form of human nature, the human capacity for knowing and loving. These capacities are inherently social. Therefore, for the ancients, humans are social animals—at least ideally, in their capacities, if not always in practice. Not all the ancients were idealists, however. There have not been many shrewder realists than Aristotle, who said that in politics we must be satisfied to see "some tincture of virtue."[1]

And this, precisely, was Hobbes's starting place. He noted that, apart from civilization, humans showed barely a tincture of virtue. In the precivilized state, "nature" shows a barbaric "war of all against all." The formal light through which Hobbes inspects experience is not historical. He does not mean that once upon a time there was a Garden of Evil ("the state of nature"), the experience of which taught humans at a specific date to value civilization. Rather, his formal light was conceptual and consisted in stressing the antisocial capacities of those human beings who lack all civilizing virtues. Aristotle noted that human beings often fall below their true perfection; that is why in their common life they show only a tincture of virtue. Hobbes's state of nature is even worse—the condition in which humans act with less than a tincture of virtue, evidencing behavior that is purely antisocial. Hobbes thought that this state is always not far from us. Indeed in our century its teeth have been bared before our eyes many times.

Still, it is much more difficult than Hobbes thinks for human beings to be purely evil in all respects. Although human evil is even more awful in its reach than he imagined, as the concentration camps, torture chambers, and gas ovens of the twentieth century have shown, there is also a broadly shared human revulsion against such evils. It is not "unnatural" for humans to be moved by the torture, pain, and death of others far away. Accordingly, the human rights revolution is slowly affecting nearly all humankind.[2] The very scholars who insist upon the sharp divide between the world of Aristotle and the world of Hobbes prize mightily what Lincoln called "the better angels of our nature" represented by higher standards of human rights performance.

The Contribution of the Catholic Whig Tradition

The Catholic Whig tradition has a crucial philosophical role to play in bridging the best of the ancient tradition with the best of the modern tradition. The modern liberal tradition has excelled in devising practical institutional protections for human rights. By contrast, the Great Tradition of the *philosophia perennis* excelled in casting light on the basic philosophical conceptions that undergird liberal institutions. The philosophies of Hobbes, Locke, and other moderns are less than adequate as philosophies. The philosophies of Aristotle, St. Thomas Aquinas, and others, however, are less than adequate with regard to the practical institutions that would incarnate their conceptions in social structures. The present task of the Catholic Whig tradition is to form a new synthesis of philosophical conceptions and practical institutions that do justice, together, to private rights and public happiness. This synthesis must join together the full actualization both of the human person and of the human community.

The Concept of "Person"

The key concepts are "person" and "community." Here the Catholic intellectual tradition, in particular, sheds special light. As the German historian of philosophy Wilhelm Windelband pointed out, the con-

17

cept of person is richer than the concept of individual and arose historically from the efforts of Catholic theologians to do justice to the theological statement that Jesus Christ is human in nature but divine in person.[3] Because theologians had to tangle with the concept of Christ's personhood, beyond his human individuality, they thought long and hard about the difference between the two concepts. It is their personhood that grounds the dignity and the rights of every man and woman.

The human person, precisely *qua* person, is a foundational source of insight and love: autonomous, sovereign, a hypostatic whole, inviolable, inalienable, an end and not only a means. The human person is called directly to union with the One in whose image each has been created. The person, therefore, can never be treated, even by the community, as a means rather than as an end. The very purpose of a true community is to nourish in its midst the full development of each person among its members. Conversely, it is in the nature of the human person—an originating source of knowing and of loving—to be in communion with others, who share in his or her knowing and loving. Knowing and loving are inherently acts of communion.

Thus, the classical view—developed by Aristotle and brought to fullness by Aquinas—holds simultaneously that, in one sense, the inherent end of personhood is communion and, in a reciprocal sense, that the inherent end of a true community is full respect for the personhood of each of its members. A human community, therefore, is *sui generis*. It is not like a hive, or a herd, or a mere collective. Each of its members is not *merely* a member, a part of the whole.[4] On the contrary, each is a whole, wholly worthy of respect in herself or himself. Each has an autonomous life of his or her own, worthy of infinite respect as a participant in God's own knowing and loving. Each is an agent of reflection and choice. Unless he or she is injuring others, the only way in which a genuine community can approach a rational person is by way of knowing and of loving—that is, through rational and civil persuasion, not through coercion, force, or systematic oppression.

Just the same, the classic Catholic tradition, even while working out wonderfully balanced accounts of person and community, tended to tip the balance toward community. Why was this? Perhaps it was that the social, familial, political, and economic institutions that would in later times enlarge the scope of personal liberty remained for many centuries unknown. Perhaps it was that existing communities were small and their survival was often threatened. (This fact is still visible in the battlements and thick walls by which the cities of ancient and medieval Europe vainly tried to repel generations of invaders.)

At least sixty times in his many works, St. Thomas Aquinas articulates one variant or another of a classic dictum that goes back as far as Aristotle: the good of the many is more godlike than the good of the individual.[5] The example that made this observation cogent to the Great Tradition is the willingness of individuals to die to defend the common good of the city. While it is easy to see why the sacrifice of self for the community seemed godlike, there is also a danger in this formulation. It may suggest to the unwary that the individual is but a means to the survival of the community. Only in extraordinary circumstances, and for a full set of sound reasons, can a community justly ask so much of its citizens.[6] Otherwise, it is wrong to imagine that the individual is always expendable, if only the social whole chooses that expedient. St. Thomas Aquinas did not himself accept this dangerously broad implication. He could not, because of his concept of the human person.

Civilization, Thomas Aquinas liked to say, is constituted by reasoned discourse. The difference between barbarism and civilization consists in this: barbaric regimes coerce their citizens; civilized regimes approach citizens through their own autonomous capacities for full consent. Persons are treated as persons only when approached through knowing and loving. For free persons, the legitimacy of government lies in the consent of the governed.[7]

The "consent of the governed" is a political principle, clearly articulated in the American Declaration of Independence of 1776. This principle flows from the reality of the human person, an autonomous creature whose essential nature consists in a capacity for reflection and choice. The only appropriate approach to such agents is through reasoned consent.[8] That truth, declared to be self-evident in 1776, was not at that time in fact self-evident to all human beings. But historical experience worldwide has made that truth increasingly self-evident to all. All the world recognizes today that any approach through tyranny, torture, or coercion—any attempt to treat human beings as parts of a mere collective, as ants in an anthill, bees in a hive, sheep in a herd, or animals on an "animal farm"—distorts and oppresses the true capacities of human persons. Any such regime is bound to be as oppressive, uncreative, and unproductive as it is illegitimate. From many sad experiences, the world has learned the hard way that the source of human creativity is the human capacity for reflective choice. Those who would build a social order worthy of human beings, therefore, must design institutions that multiply acts of reflective choice.

One of the contributions of modern thought to ancient thought, therefore, is sharper and more sustained attention to the nature and the rights of the human person. Where ancient and medieval societies tipped the balance toward the common good, modern societies have placed compensating weights—and sometimes more than compensating weights—on the side of the person. Modern institutions make this new emphasis practical, concrete, and consequential.

But where should one draw the line? How should one strike a balance? This debate is more than academic. Push too far in the direction of solidarity, and the outcome is the totalitarian collective. Push too far in the direction of the individual, and the outcome is egotism, moral relativism (subjectivism), and a war of all against all. Even among thinkers determined to avoid both extremes, how exactly to do justice both to person and to community is not easily discernible—not in daily family life, not in the institutions of religion, not in political action, and not in the business corporation. Thinkers of a moderate bent wish to honor both the person and the community—both the needs of individuals and the needs of social harmony. But how, where, and in what degree?

My aim now is not to answer that question in the abstract. Instead, I take a hint from Tocqueville in *Democracy in America*, who suggests that the terms of the ancient debate between the person and the community (between *personalism* and *solidarism*, as certain Europeans said in the 1930s) have been changed by the American experience. The New World is different from the Old World. What we mean by "person" is different here, as well as what we mean by "community." And the *Novus Ordo* has accordingly suggested a fresh historical solution to an ancient conundrum.

Tocqueville: The New World Symphony

Alexis de Tocqueville was not only an acute observer; he was also a social scientist of the first rank. And he formulated from what he observed in what he took to be the first people to embody the new order of the ages the first law of the "new science of politics." His purpose was to alert Europe to a new tide in human history, a tide deep and wide and directed by Providence, that would soon, or eventually, sweep the whole world.[9] He meant the tide of a new kind of democracy, a democratic republic with an effective respect for the singular human person. A new kind of political-economic-moral order was rising, under the hand of Providence, he thought, and perhaps the most striking thing about this new order is that in it "men have in our time carried to the highest perfection the art of pursuing in common the object of common desires, and have applied this new technique to the greatest number of purposes."[10] Here Tocqueville called attention to a new reality, which can fairly be described neither as individualistic nor, quite, as constituting a full community. This new reality is a new form of social life: the voluntary association.

In America, Tocqueville observed, when citizens discerned new needs or purposes, they voluntarily formed committees or other informal organizations to meet them. What in France citizens turned to the state to do for them, Tocqueville exclaimed, and what in Great Britain they turned to the aristocracy to do, in America they formed their own associations to accomplish. Thus they built great universities, museums, and art galleries; sent missionaries to the antipodes; raised funds for the disabled; put up public monuments; fed and clothed victims of natural disasters, and the like.[11] This new form of social life—never total enough to constitute a fully defined community, but far beyond the power of individuals alone—called for a new "knowledge of association."

This new knowledge of association, Tocqueville explains,

> is the mother of all other forms of knowledge; on its progress depends that of all the others. . . . Among laws controlling human societies there is one more precise and clearer, it seems to me, than all the others. If men are to remain civilized or to become civilized, the art of association must develop and improve among them at the same speed as equality of conditions spreads.[12]

Why association? Because inherent in respect for the human person is respect for the reflectively chosen forms of association that persons create to pursue their common interests. To constitute a people out of mere masses or mere mobs, such freely, rationally chosen associations are indispensable.[13]

In an important sense (not only a historical sense, as actually happened in the United States), such freely chosen associations are prior to the state. They are prior philosophically and practically: philosophically, because they ground the social nature of the human person in reflective and voluntary social life, duly proportioned to the human bodily need of proximity, voice, and active participation; practically, because human beings need immediate participation in the forming of social consent and they also need social protection, lest in their solitary individual selves they stand naked before the power of an omnipotent state.

In short, mediating associations or mediating institutions, as these voluntarily formed local structures are technically called, are crucial forms of human sociality, and they are prior to the formation of a national society.[14] They are defenses against the state. They are also natural expressions of concrete, fleshly human sociality. Before humans are citizens of states, they are active participants in society.

As Jacques Maritain has stressed, society is a far larger and more vital reality than state.[15] Only a densely active society with many vital civic associations is sufficiently defended against the state, whose tendencies have historically been tyrannous. Only a society with many vital associations fully expresses the social nature of the person. The new science of association, therefore, meets two basic needs of human nature: one positive, one negative. The social nature of humans gives rise to associations not only because individuals need protection from abuse but also because they have a positive need for participation and self-expression.[16] In addition, in a way entirely appropriate to the human person, associations come into being through personal consent.

Tocqueville is surely correct: the principle of association is, in fact, the first law of democracy. Without vital mediating institutions, intermediate between the naked individual and the state, democracy has no muscular social fiber; it is a void within which a mere mob is blown about by demagoguery. The strength of a people, as distinguished from a mob, lies in its capacities for voluntarily forming multiple associations of self-government and social purpose on its own.[17] In that case, the social life of a people is rich, complex, and strong before the question of a national state even arises.

Even President Gorbachev appears to have grasped this. To make Soviet society creative, he must free Soviet persons (at least a little) through *glasnost,* allowing creative and reflective intellect to flourish. To derive legitimacy and creative cooperation from all the people, he must reshape Soviet institutions through *perestroika.* To break through the stranglehold of Communist party members over every sclerotic institution of Soviet life, he must go as far as he dares to empower the creativity of individual citizens. The source of dynamic power in any human community, in short, is the creativity locked within the capacities of individual human persons for insight and choice.

Latin Americans sometimes charge that the Anglo-American liberal tradition is excessive in its emphasis upon the individual and deficient in its philosophy of community.[18] That charge is not quite accurate; still, for the sake of argument, let me accept its burden. Suppose that it is true that on these two points the *philosophy* of the liberal society is inferior to, say, Catholic social thought. From that it does not follow that the institutional praxis of the liberal society is inferior to the institutional praxis of existing Catholic social orders. It is at least conceivable that liberal societies such as West Germany,

Great Britain, France, and the United States pay a more just respect to the rights of persons on the one hand and on the other hand to the building up of intermediate social bodies through reflection and choice than do some existing Catholic countries. Explicit philosophy and institutional practice do not always coincide. Indeed, practice may often be better than philosophy. This was the judgment of Jacques Maritain in his *Reflections on America*—that American practices are better, deeper, richer than American ideology.[19]

Let me further propose the Novak rule of philosophical interpretation. Philosophers (and theologians) often stress in their writings exactly what their cultures lack and are silent about solid habits readily taken for granted. Thus, in Great Britain, where social conformity has long been in fashion and where individuals are supremely sensitive to others around them and have internalized a sort of social conscience, British philosophers speak incessantly about the individual. By contrast, in Italy philosophers speak incessantly about *communitá*—while practicing an almost medieval and princely self-assertion and exhibiting a fiercely proud individualism bordering on idiosyncrasy. Compare in those two countries the social practice of boarding a bus. In London, citizens patiently and respectfully queue up in social awareness. In Rome, boarding a bus is one of the world's wildest adventures in laissez faire and one of its most sensuous experiences. In London, where philosophers praise individualism, individuals defer to others; in Rome, where philosophers praise community, it's every man for himself. The Novak rule anticipates this turn.

The Codefinition of Person and Community

In sum, those who in the long run trust realism and the lessons of vivid human experience—and who hold to first principles such as the "self-evident truth" that persons are appropriately respected solely when their native capacities for reflection and choice are permitted free play—seem to have been vindicated by history. "The God who gave us life gave us liberty," Thomas Jefferson said.[20] He made the same point in the text of the Declaration of Independence, for which he wanted posterity to remember him: "That all men are created equal, and endowed by their Creator with certain unalienable Rights." None of the rights he had in mind are American rights; they are human rights. They inhere in persons—they are the properties proper to human persons—because they were conferred on each directly by the Creator, who made all human persons in His image. Catholic thought adds further that as the proper life of God is insight

23

and love, so also is that life proper to human persons. As God is a person, so are humans.

It is the distinctive achievement of the modern Catholic Whig tradition to have added to the classical perception of the primacy (in certain respects) of the community the modern perception of the primacy (in other respects) of the person. This achievement permits unparalleled social concern for the rights, liberties, and dignity of human persons, *qua* persons (that is, *not* because of their opinions, beliefs, religion, ethnicity, or race). But it also nourishes the achievement of a vastly larger number of voluntary associations, a higher degree of voluntary social cooperation, a broader base of love and gratitude for the commonwealth, and a more explicitly consensual national community than was known in ancient or medieval times.

Creating new social systems—or reconstituting old ones—to show historically unparalleled respect both for individual persons and for the common good is not merely a possibility. Some three dozen societies on this planet (none of them, of course, saintly or likely to be mistaken for the Kingdom of God) have actually shown such respect, in their institutions and in their daily practice. Far from being perfect, each of these societies has left much to be done before liberty and justice for all are fully served. Such societies do, however, afford protections for basic rights more broadly and efficaciously than was ever done before, in any traditional, premodern, precapitalist, and prerepublican society.

To my way of thinking, the Whig tradition—and particularly the Catholic Whig tradition—offers the world's best statement of philosophical principles and practical guidelines, concerning how and why free citizens should shape new societies worthy of their human rights and ordered liberties. Such societies, to secure these rights, must give primacy to community. But to build true and authentic communities, these societies must give primacy to persons. Both forms of primacy are important. Each is necessary for the other's definition—and for the other's flourishing.

To secure the rights of the person, give primacy to community. To build a genuinely human community, give primacy to the person. Such is the Catholic Whig tradition, tutored by the experience of the Americas and shocked by the terrors of the twentieth century. And such, now, is most of the world's agenda.

4
The Virtue of Enterprise

In the two preceding chapters, three fundamental principles of the Catholic Whig tradition have emerged: ordered liberty, person, and community. They bring us to a fourth principle of Catholic Whig thought, one that bears directly upon economic life: the moral virtue of enterprise. Catholic Whig thought proclaims the primacy of morals over politics and economics. The reason is that any social system dedicated to human liberty must recognize the moral activism and responsibility inherent in the use of liberty. In a free society, individual persons exercise far greater liberty of economic action than in any totalitarian, authoritarian, or traditional society. Their moral responsibilities are correspondingly greater. *Ubi libertas, ibi iudicium*—wherever there is liberty, accountability follows. Insofar as the free society increases the scope for liberty, so it enlarges the burdens (or, better, the joys) of morality.

A Whig Theory of Morals

Still, it is perhaps too Kantian to think that morality means solely obligations, burdens, and responsibilities. The Whigs side rather more with the Greeks: true morality is the exercise of ever-larger capacities for action and belongs as such in the realm of joy and beauty. For Aristotle, to *act well* is the very definition of happiness. For Whigs, happiness is deeper than feelings and may persist even under feelings of pain or dread. Those who act with courage, for example, may experience not pleasant feelings but an inner sense of doing the right thing, at the right time, for the right reason, in the right way. To be happy, one should not take feelings as one's guide; on the contrary, one should set one's moral compass to acting with integrity and train one's feelings to delight in that: first the substance of the act, then the feeling.

What do Whigs mean, then, by morality? They mean the exercise of fundamental human capacities, to the limits (virtually infinite) of their deployment. They mean the full development of human potentialities. They mean the beauty and exhilaration of large and great-souled actions and of fidelity to small details ("God is in the details").

They mean human consciousness at a high pitch of attentiveness, noticing, alertness—and human will at a high level of discrimination and choice. To be human is to reflect and to choose. To be moral is to exercise these capacities frequently, with pleasure, and to the fullest extent attainable. A wise person exercises reflection and choice as often as possible every day, deliberately extending them even into such reflexive acts as sipping water, walking, combing hair, or conversing. *Be attentive!* is the dynamo of moral action.

Moral imperatives arise wherever human beings act in politics and economic life, in the family, and even in solitude. The primacy of morals derives from human liberty. Still, it was not until 1776 that two new lessons were learned, from Adam Smith, about the scope and consequences of liberty in the economic order.[1] First, human beings *can* create national wealth in a sustained and systematic way; they thus inherit thereafter responsibility for poverty. If no one can create wealth, then poverty is simply a fact; but if a society knows how to create wealth and does not, then poverty is immoral. Second, the cause of the wealth of nations is the human mind: that is to say, human creativity. The ancients and medievals had the honor of discovering many important truths about politics (as in Aristotle's *Politics*, St. Thomas's *De Regimine Principum*, Dante's *De Monarchia*, Machiavelli's *The Prince*, and many others). The great discovery of the modern period is economics. Human liberty can be extended not only throughout political life but also throughout economic life. So thought the Whigs.

Ironically, the second of these truths—that the cause of the wealth of nations is the human mind—is a moral truth. It implanted the moral code at the heart of all economic activity. (I say "ironically," because soon after Adam Smith's discovery, economists began to treat their new field of inquiry as a science rather than as a branch of moral philosophy, even though Adam Smith had clearly thought of it as a subdiscipline of moral philosophy.) In this spirit, even John Stuart Mill wrote in his *Principles of Political Economy*, one of the most widely reprinted textbooks of the late nineteenth century, that economics is a moral art, which he compared with other arts necessary to the statesman.[2] In Smith's eyes, economics has to do with the proper arrangement of society, in accord with the system of natural liberty, that leads to the ever-improving wealth of nations and the equitable distribution of that wealth. Thus economics is both a moral art and a social art, addressing the proper and just arrangement of social institutions, oriented toward maximizing personal economic creativity, for the sake of the common economic whole.

Although most economists after Smith increasingly detached

economics from moral philosophy in the name of science, the great Heinrich Pesch, S.J., in his multivolumed works on the social economy, did not.[3] He discerned clearly that the dynamic of every economic system is the energy generated by the moral habits of its citizens. Economic activities spring from human liberty and thus from moral agency. A passive population, exercising liberty hardly at all, displays a diminished range of economic activities, compared with a more industrious population. Moreover, the kinds of virtues and the kinds of vices that characterize a population define the profile of its economic limits. Consider, for example, two peoples of different moral cultures working within the same economic system—the Chinese in Malaysia, evangelical Protestants in Honduras, and the Japanese in Brazil. In all three cases, these small minorities are spectacularly successful within economies in which others succeed much less well. The specific characteristics of two or more different moral cultures commonly generate different economic results even within the same system.[4]

Although after Adam Smith economics developed as a science separate from the humanities and moral philosophy, that long trend is now changing. During the course of this century, and especially since the end of World War II, more than a hundred new economic experiments have been conducted all around the world: Socialist, traditionalist, capitalist. One factor glaringly apparent from these experiments is the diverse impact of various moral cultures upon economic performance. The peoples of the world are not wholly interchangeable. While economic reality is indeed a field of scientific study and scientific specialization, it is also a humanistic field. One of its absolutely basic variables is the human person—his aims, actions, motives, and choices. At its very base lies human liberty, used differently by different persons and different cultures. History clearly shows that the uses of human liberty affect not only the inner moral form of economic activity but also economic results. As Adam Smith's *Inquiry* predicted, human beings *can* extend the sphere of liberty into economic activities, by studying the causes of wealth and acting accordingly. In addition, the wealth of nations derives from a specific use of human liberty—namely, to create—and on this measure, culture differs from culture, system from system.

Here we should pause to emphasize that economic reality is *inherently* social. Through economic activities, citizens fulfill one another's material needs and join together to improve their common material good. Exchange is of the essence of economic activity. Indeed, some early Fathers of the church saw in commerce among the various nations, each with different resources and different advantages, a metaphor for the interdependence of the human race.[5] Looked at religiously, international economic activities, based upon voluntary transactions, represent a humble and earthly image of the unity of humankind in its daily activities.[6] Out of the many comes a certain interdependence. One nation excels in the production of wines, another one in the production of wool. This nation has great mineral resources, while that one has none. In their variety, the nations meet each other's needs. Through economic life, their interdependence becomes visible to the naked eye, a metaphor for their deeper unity in the system of natural liberty.

This natural liberty, in turn, is the wellspring of enterprise and creativity—the cause of economic prosperity, the engine of development. Since the driving force of economic prosperity is moral agency, the primacy of morals in economic life is vindicated. The name of this moral agency within the economic realm is enterprise.

The Right to Personal Economic Initiative

The answer to Adam Smith's question, "What is the cause of the wealth of nations?" may be given in a single word—in Latin, *caput;* the human mind, wit, invention. The cause of the wealth of nations is the creativity of the human person. The person is the originating source of invention, enterprise, and economic dynamism. Smith's example for this was the pin factory: the invention of a machine (and a new way of organizing labor) to produce pins at a rate incredibly faster than individual craftsmen alone had ever before been able to produce them.[7] This invention generated enormous new wealth, and it also made pins available for the first time to the poor. As Friedrich von Hayek once pointed out, capitalism did little for duchesses, who already had silk stockings, but a great deal for poor and working class women who soon had silk stockings too.

Practically all the little things of daily life that have lightened our days—things that we have around us and use every day—are fruits of economic creativity. A concise definition of capitalism is the system designed to nourish the creativity of the human subject or to nourish, in Smith's phrase, "skill, dexterity and judgment."[8] It is a system centered upon mind. The heart of capitalism is *caput*, human wit. The ordinary name for economic creativity is enterprise.

Pope John Paul II has greatly advanced Catholic social teaching, therefore, by grounding its economic viewpoint in the story of creation in the Book of Genesis. This he has done in his encyclicals *Laborem Exercens* and *Sollicitudo Rei Socialis.*

Moreover, the pope has linked the ancient concept of creativity to the contemporary concept of enterprise and initiative.[9] This is a very important step. He goes so far as to call "personal economic enterprise" a fundamental human right, which he paired with the fundamental human right of liberty of conscience. Like liberty of conscience, the holy father roots this right in the subjectivity of the human person, made in the image of the Creator, and says that sins against this right destroy that image of God in humans and wreak human devastation:

> Experience shows us that the denial of this right, or its limitation in the name of an alleged "equality" of everyone in society, diminishes, or in practice absolutely destroys the spirit of initiative, that is to say *the creative subjectivity of the citizen.* As a consequence, there arises, not so much a true equality as a "leveling down." In the place of creative initiative there appears passivity, dependence and submission to the bureaucratic apparatus which, as the only "ordering" and "decision-making" body—if not also the "owner"—of the entire totality of goods and the means of production, puts everyone in a position of almost absolute dependence, which is similar to the traditional dependence of the worker-proletarian in capitalism. This provokes a sense of frustration or desperation and predisposes people to opt out of national life, impelling many to emigrate and also favoring a form of "psychological" emigration.[10]

Clearly, the exercise of personal economic enterprise is close to the moral center of the human person. By declaring such exercise to be a right, Pope John Paul II leaves Catholic social thought with a further question. If personal economic enterprise is a fundamental right, in what precisely does its exercise consist? What *is* enterprise? If it is a central capacity of personhood—the image of God in us—to exercise it must also be a duty. Not to exercise it appears to be a fault.

But what is enterprise? If I am not mistaken, in Spanish the verb *emprender* encompasses several meanings: to start a business as well as to act with an enterprising spirit. The important note is that the latter can become a habit, a moral virtue. This virtue can be taught. And a social system can be constructed to support it.

When have we ever heard in church or learned from a text of moral theology that personal economic enterprise is a necessary moral virtue? Or received instruction in how to practice it? Or learned to criticize social systems in the light of how well, or how badly, they nourish and promote personal economic enterprise? Does any catechism teach even so much as the basic conceptual definition of this virtue?

The explanation for this still undeveloped part of Catholic social teaching is that this virtue is a relatively new one, given special prominence by a new stage of human social development. Every form of society vivifies, among its citizens, a special selection of virtues. The virtues of Athens differed from the virtues of Sparta; even today, those of Madrid differ from those of Rome or Bonn or London or Minneapolis. Every society consists of its own distinctive institutions, manners, arrangements, customs, practices, and habits. Thus, Tocqueville (one of the greatest Catholic Whigs) observed correctly that republican societies require a long education in liberty to prepare their citizens for the new responsibilities inherent in self-government.[11] Republican societies call forth new virtues in the political order as well as in the economic order.

Let us consider how this works. Today, traditional habits appropriate to living under tyrants or even under the old aristocratic feudal system have to yield to the habits appropriate to self-government. Democracy is not only a form of government but a new way of living that requires a new way of thinking, feeling, and organizing one's inner life. It demands new sets of human virtues. If citizens cannot govern their own inner lives, how can they mutually govern one another in social life? A democratic revolution is moral or not a revolution at all. Republican institutions require republican virtues. Among these are initiative, a sense of personal responsibility, and skill in forming associations to fulfill multiple social purposes. Free citizens must take responsibility for nearly every aspect of their lives. They cannot await the benevolence of others. Under self-government, they are themselves sovereign; *they* become the ones responsible for everything.

Like a new political order, a new economic order also demands a new set of moral virtues. Like a feudal political order, the traditional economic order was largely state run, mercantilist, and relatively uninventive. It required virtues appropriate to a feudal order. A free economic order, however, requires a new set of virtues parallel to those appropriate to a republican political order. The centerpiece of these new virtues, close to being "the form of all the (economic) virtues," is personal economic enterprise. This virtue is rooted in God-given capacities for creativity.

Like practical wisdom, personal economic enterprise is a virtue of the practical intellect. It is at once an intellectual and a moral virtue. It is an intellectual virtue because the essence of economic enterprise is an act of discernment, an alertness, a noticing. It is a moral virtue because it falls under the formality of advancing the common good (particularly, but not solely, the material common good) of society. Enterprise is, further, not a solitary act; it is relational. Most of the time, it advances human interdependence.

Thus, personal economic enterprise is in its essence intellectual, moral, and social. As it is the cause of the wealth of nations, so, in aggregate, it is ordered to the common good. Indeed, to exercise enterprise in an antisocial way is, over time, self-defeating. For to tear down the tissues of mutual trust, mutual confidence, and mutual cooperation—on all of which general prosperity depends—is to arouse defensive reactions in others and to lead society into a war of all against all. When moral vices eat away its rootage, a social system collapses in ruins upon the enterprises of all.

We have now approached the concept of personal economic enterprise from the outside in, so to speak, by classifying it among the other virtues as intellectual, moral, and social. But what is it in itself? First of all, like practical wisdom, personal economic enterprise is a capacity for *insight*.[12] In its first moment, it is the habit of discerning new possibilities. This insight may consist in imagining new products and new services not now available. It may also consist in new, better, or more efficient methods of producing or distributing them. The person of economic enterprise, like the person of practical wisdom, is habitually alert to possibilities for action that those without the habit commonly overlook. In its second moment, the virtue of enterprise consists in realizing one's creative insights in the world of fact. Just as practical wisdom leads to doing, practical enterprise leads to creating. Whereas practical wisdom is ordered to acting well, economic enterprise is ordered to creating well. In this respect, economic enterprise is a species of art—a commercial art, an industrial art, an entrepreneurial art, one of the arts of human service. It is, then, "a humanism on empirical grounds."[13] The scholastics defined an art as *recta ratio factibilium*, reason ordered to making things well.[14]

From an economic point of view, enterprise is the single most important cause of the wealth of nations. It introduces new goods and services to benefit the human race. In creating new markets and new reasons for exchange, it generates new jobs and raises standards of living. Enterprise is the dynamic force in business activity, the principle of change.

Enterprise may also work by generating new savings. In this sense, it sometimes conserves wealth that otherwise would have been squandered. An American automobile company, for example, spends hundreds of millions of dollars annually for paint for all the automobiles it produces. An enterprising and courageous executive closely studied the company's traditional methods for purchasing paint. He found that contracts were written with large national suppliers and then the paint was distributed to auto plants all around the United

States. Looking still more closely, the new executive saw possibilities for immense savings by decentralizing the contracts and allowing each plant to accept bids from local suppliers. Despite fierce traditionalist resistance, his plan was carried through. The result was greater satisfaction throughout the system, since the use of local suppliers resulted in lower transport costs and greater local control. The company also reaped a financial savings of nearly 15 percent. On a base of many hundreds of millions of dollars annually, a 15 percent savings was highly significant. These savings accrue to society at large, insofar as these unsquandered funds are turned to more creative uses, by allowing either prices to be cut or productive new investments to be made.

In another example, new inventions and new methods allowed agricultural productivity in the United States to double between 1963 and 1975. By 1988 it had doubled again. Whereas in 1900 some 40 percent of the U.S. work force was engaged in producing food for the nation, today only about 2 percent is so engaged.[15]

Moreover, new inventions have made industries and industrial products today much smaller, cleaner, and cheaper.[16] The first computer at the Massachusetts Institute of Technology in 1939 filled a room. Today, personal computers in millions of homes contain more computational power than the one at MIT. Electronic calculators, not long ago the size of typewriters, are now thin enough to carry in a billfold. Radios, once the size of a trunk, now fit in a shirt pocket and produce a much higher fidelity of sound. Through such sustained inventiveness, quality has risen, size has shrunk, and prices have declined. All these benefits spring from personal economic enterprise.

Finally, economic enterprise plays two other important social roles. First, it is a magnificent generator of employment. Second, its main strength is that it is *personal* and allows millions of families to launch their own businesses. The creativity of such persons may be expressed in economic matters rather than in clay, or oil paint, or music, but they are artists nonetheless. The money that they invest to cover start-up costs is placed at risk. Their art has consequences for their economic well-being. We can be certain that they will need every ounce of enterprising discernment they can muster to avoid squandering their resources unwisely. This is the spur of their invention and their willingness to work. The problem for socialism, a left-wing American economist has written, is, Who will stay up all night with a sick cow?[17] When the cow is one's own, this problem disappears. The virtue of enterprise teaches its possessors the risks, the difficulties, and the satisfactions of becoming masters of their own economic destiny.

Economic enterprise too is inherently social: producing goods and services that no one values is pointless. A person of economic enterprise is driven to study the needs and wants of others. To be successful, the enterprising person must be, to a remarkable degree, other regarding, because focusing on others is inherent in economic activities. Such a focus falls far short of Christian charity or even altruism; it is not completely selfless. But it is, just the same, not a bad school in the elementary disciplines of consideration for needs and wants other than one's own. Sound human relations with one's fellow workers, suppliers, customers, and others is a proven road to economic success. The lack of these engenders hostile resistance, rejection, and social alienation.

If enterprise is an intellectual and moral virtue, we need to know how to learn and how to teach it. Instruction in enterprise consists in awakening to one's own creative capacities, to the many unmet needs of fellow citizens, and to the openness of economic possibilities surrounding us. Yet instruction in the virtue of enterprise consists, too, in alertness to social obstacles to enterprise. If all processes of legal incorporation are heavily controlled, regulated, and taxed by state authorities, for example, enterprise may be slaughtered in its infancy.[18] According to Pope John Paul II, states that oppress personal economic enterprise violate not only a fundamental human right but also the image of the Creator endowed in every human subject. Such societies damage the common good of all and doom their citizens to stagnant, uncreative, and spiritually alienating economies—as the pope says, "leading many citizens even to emigrate from their native lands."

Catholic social teaching holds that personal economic initiative is a fundamental human right. It holds, further, that to exercise that right is to fulfill the image of God inherent in every man and woman. It follows, then, that teachers of Catholic social thought must awaken people to the God-given capacities within them. They must instruct them in how to practice the virtue of enterprise and how to avoid the vices that would destroy or disfigure it. They must show them examples of what to do, and what not to do, in fulfilling the potential within them.

Furthermore, teachers of Catholic social thought should lead the way in discerning those practices of governments or other establishments that stifle, suffocate, or otherwise repress the daily practice of personal economic enterprise. They should condemn statist practices and customs that block the flowering of creative talents in economic enterprise; that keep markets open solely to established firms and existing monopolies and closed to all others; that make legal incorporation a lengthy, expensive, and corrupt procedure; that fail to establish institutions that supply credit to poor, humble, or unknown persons; that fail to recognize how God distributes creative economic talents to all social classes and all human beings. Teachers of Catholic social thought should also censure oppressive authorities that excessively tax or overregulate economic activities in such a way that new firms cannot establish even a foothold. Teachers of Catholic social thought should make certain that the ways of enterprise are open especially to the poor.

The enemies of personal economic initiative are many, powerful, and well established in many traditionalist societies. This is why traditionalist societies are static: by punishing those citizens who show creative economic initiative, they constrict the horizons of the common good and thus punish all other citizens as well.

Conclusion

Many other moral and intellectual virtues must flourish in abundance if a free and creative economy is to prosper. In an economic system where dishonesty is frequent and corruption rampant, where egotism inspires contempt for fellow workers and customers, and where on all sides hostility and defensiveness reign, there is pitifully little room for creativity. In such air, free creative enterprise cannot breathe. If any economic system is to flourish, such vices must be replaced by their opposing virtues. Human vices poison economic vitality. Moral virtues not only lessen economic costs but enhance the free and thriving exercise of practical reason, hope, and creative risk.

For a regime anywhere on earth to exhibit full moral perfection is, of course, beyond human fallibility. Whig realism—Catholic realism—always leads us to expect less than that. In economics, as in politics, if we may paraphrase Aristotle, the wise must be satisfied with a tincture of virtue. Building an economy for saints anywhere on earth is useless. There are too few of them. The only realistic possibility is to build an economy for sinners—the only moral majority.

Nonetheless, the broader the circle of virtue in any economic system, the more creative, prosperous, and pleasant work within that economy is likely to be. Conversely, the more virulent the fever of human vices that rage within it, the more defensive, suspicious, self-defeating, and unhealthy an economy is likely to be.

It is crucial, therefore, to understand that human capital includes moral capital, as well as intellectual: skills of the human heart, as well as skills of hand. In economic life, as everywhere else in human life, the primacy of morals is a fundamental, demonstrable law of human prosperity. The primacy of morals is an empirical, as well as a philosophical, principle. It is subject to falsification. The consequences of violating it show up in history rather rapidly. Laziness, dishonesty, coercion, unfettered greed, and other moral vices eat like moths at the fabric of economic success.

To end these reflections on a downward bent, however, would be wrong. The fact that human beings are made in the image of the Creator means that every human person, during his or her lifetime, can create more than he or she will consume.[19] This is the ground of all hope for economic progress. No one guarantees that we will be creative rather than destructive. To be so, however, is our vocation, our right, and our responsibility. We have a chance—all of us, collectively and individually—to act creatively. We have a chance, a kick at the goal. That is all a free woman or man can ask.

It is important, too, not to lose sight of our goal: to liberate the poor from poverty. But how can we do this realistically? Human beings are not saints. How can we devise structures that actually help the poor—not merely rhetorically, but in practice—in a world as imperfect and often even as immoral as historical experience shows this world to be? We must turn now to the question of structures.

5
Structures of Virtue,
Structures of Sin

How can we best help the poor no longer to be poor? Pope John Paul II supplied an answer at CEPAL (The Economic Commission for Latin America) on his visit to Chile in 1987. The best way to help the poor is systematic: through a system that creates economic growth from the bottom up, a system that creates jobs for the poor. Every able-bodied poor person needs a job and must become an economic activist.

A job, the pope said, gives a poor person two advantages. First, it enables him to purchase goods for his own needs and those of his dear ones. Second, it gives him a sense of achievement, dignity, self-reliance, and social position. Work gives an adult man or woman a sense of participation and accomplishment.[1]

But how can Latin America create 70 million new jobs before the year 2005, just for the 70 million youngsters already born and now under the age of fifteen? Each year from now to 2005 A.D. a cohort of these youngsters will be turning sixteen and seeking work.

The task ahead is a *social* task. It requires a creative social *system*. It requires "personal economic initiative," that spark of enterprise that Pope John Paul II sees as necessary "for the common good."[2] This personal economic initiative is, the pope says, a fundamental human right, endowed in all by the Creator, in the depths of human personality. God made every man and woman in His image. Each has a vocation to be creative.

To help the poor is to help each poor person exercise his or her God-given right to personal economic initiative—to be creative. To do so is a social task. It is an urgent task.

But what "system" will do this? How should we think about "system"? I want to stress the importance of three realities: self-interest, sin, and the virtues of liberty and creativity.

A Republic for Sinners

Several years ago, a group of priests from Latin America traveled north to a university in the United States for a seminar on economics.

For nearly a week, they heard lectures and took part in discussions with North American economists. At the last session of what had been a happy seminar, one of the priests arose to say that his colleagues had assembled the night before and asked him to make a statement on their behalf.

"We have," he said, "greatly enjoyed this week. We have learned a great deal. We see very well that capitalism is the most effective means of producing wealth, and even that it distributes wealth more broadly and more evenly than the economic systems we see in Latin America. But we still think that capitalism is an immoral system."

To those who believe that an economic system is a means to a larger end, the judgment of these priests seems very strange. If the purpose of an economic system is to produce wealth abundantly and to distribute it broadly and if capitalism does both these things, then capitalism would seem to be fulfilling its inherent purposes. It would seem to be not only moral but morally superior. In what way can it be thought to be immoral?

No doubt these priests were thinking that capitalism is based upon self-interest; but in their view, self-interest is an immoral motive. They believe that capitalism depends upon an ethic of "having," but they favor an ethic of "being." They held that capitalism depends upon, and encourages, human tendencies toward selfishness, acquisitiveness, and even greed, whereas, in their eyes, a truly moral system would encourage habits of unselfishness, cooperation, and concern for the common good. After a full week of study, therefore, these priests were prepared to conclude that, although capitalism more effectively produces material goods than other systems, it does not nourish the moral and spiritual side of human life. In their view, capitalism is a system based on cynicism, corrupting the very springs of moral development.

Is the judgment of these priests a true judgment? Behind that, what *kind* of judgment is it? That is, upon what sort of evidence is it based?

This judgment does not seem to be empirical. It does not assert that, on the whole, the moral life of citizens in traditional societies, such as those of Latin America, is superior to the moral life of the citizens of capitalist countries, such as those of North America, Europe, or Japan. In venturing such an empirical hypothesis, one could try to gather evidence to confirm it or disprove it. But that is not what the Latin American priests were doing. They did not mean that a survey of the people of Argentina, say, and a survey of a corresponding section of the United States would indicate that the existing moral habits visible in the Argentines were superior to the moral habits of Americans. Although they might have been offering such a hypothesis, I don't think they were.

Rather, the judgment they were making was based upon a deductive analysis. During their entire week of economic discussions, the term "self-interest" recurred again and again, until it seemed to them to be the fundamental concept of a capitalist economy. They understood self-interest to indicate both a radical form of selfishness, on the one hand, and, on the other hand, an expression of materialistic interests. "Self" and "interest"—both halves of "self-interest"—bothered them. They preferred *un*selfishness and *dis*interestedness. The philosophical foundation of capitalist theory seemed to them to rest upon both excessive individualism and practical materialism. This merely logical analysis led them to pronounce the system immoral.

The way of thinking about human nature articulated by these priests is quite traditional. They wish to build a social order based on reason, the social virtues, and the Christian way of life. If human beings had not been deeply wounded by sin, no doubt such a project could succeed. Indeed, the experiment of the Holy Roman Empire was built exactly upon these lines. The founding ideals of the Holy Roman Empire were rooted in concepts of natural law and Christian virtue. If this experiment had truly resulted in ending tyranny and torture, perhaps contemporary institutions of constitutional democracy and human rights would not have been necessary. If the Holy Roman Empire had resulted in changing the conditions of the poor, so that they would no longer be poor, then no doubt the institutions of modern capitalism would not have been invented. If the Holy Roman Empire had truly resulted in respect for the human conscience, in religious toleration, and in genuine pluralism, then no doubt contemporary experiments in religious liberty and cultural pluralism would not have occurred. Sadly, however, the experiment of the Holy Roman Empire, whatever its glories, did not result in the liberation of peoples—either politically or economically, or in conscience, information, and ideas.

For this reason, a new experiment was undertaken toward the end of the eighteenth century, particularly in the Western Hemisphere, this "hemisphere of liberty" as German Arciniegas, the Colombian historian, puts it. The starting place of this new experiment was a simple empirical observation that may be tested at all times and in all places: every single human being sometimes sins. Any person of basic honesty must admit, in an examination of conscience, that at times we have betrayed our own ideals, done what we ought not have done, and left undone things that we ought to

39

have done. The task for a political philosophy that would seek genuine and effective human liberation, therefore, is not the task of building a system designed for angels or saints. The task is rather to build a system that will work for sinners.

Anyone who would build a social system aimed at liberation must deal with human beings as we are. "If men were angels," James Madison wrote, "no government would be necessary."[3] But human beings are not angels. Any effective social system must therefore be designed for sinners. Indeed, not only a majority is at stake; the reach of sin is universal (excepting only our Lady and our Lord).

The framers of the Constitution of the United States were well aware that all structures built by human beings for human beings are "sinful structures." Although some Latin American theologians of today have made the conception of sinful structures current, they are by no means the inventors of the concept. The idea that all human structures are sinful structures is at least as old as the Constitution of the United States. The underlying theory of this Constitution is well expressed in the best handbook for practical revolutionaries ever written, *The Federalist*, consisting of essays by Alexander Hamilton, James Madison, and John Jay and designed to persuade their fellow citizens of 1787 and 1788 that the Constitution of the United States ought to be ratified by the people, whose will it represented.

The framers wanted to build a *novus ordo* that would secure "liberty and justice for all." Their main aim was liberation. Actually, they had in mind *three* liberations: political liberation; economic liberation; and moral, cultural, and religious liberation.

Still, they had a rather specific concept of liberty. They did not intend by "liberty" what the French mean by *liberté*. They expressly did not mean libertinism, or mere voluntarism, or the unleasing of naked passions, or freedom from restraint, or even liberty apart from reason. On the contrary, they spoke of "ordered liberty," as Pope John Paul II expressly recalled when greeting President Reagan on the first day of the pope's visit to the United States at Miami in 1987.

Indeed, on the seal of the United States, where today one finds the inscription *Novus Ordo Seclorum* ("The New Order of the Ages"), an earlier version of the inscription, almost selected by the framers, bore simply the word *"virtue."* As James Madison said;

> Is there no virtue among us? If there be not, we are in a wretched situation. No theoretical checks, no form of government, can render us secure. To suppose any form of government will secure liberty or happiness without any virtue in the people, is a chimerical idea.[4]

What, then, in the view of the framers, is "the new order of the ages"? The underlying principle of this new order is the fact of sin (not in its supernatural but in its natural effects). To build a republic designed for sinners, then, is the indispensable task. Its accomplishment, accordingly, requires both a limited government and a system of checks and balances throughout the entire social system. Limited government is required to prevent tyranny, for even the most benign philosopher-king must sometimes be tempted to tyranny or to torture—always, of course, for "the common good." It is always so. Therefore, government must be limited, and its powers precisely determined by a written constitution: thus far, and no farther. The rights of humans are not well protected merely by "parchment barriers," and therefore power must be checked by power, interest by interest:

> Ambition must be made to counteract ambition . . . the constant aim is to divide and arrange the several offices in such a manner as that each may be a check on the other—that the private interest of every individual may be a sentinel over the public rights.[5]

The meaning of "interest" has changed since the end of the eighteenth century. This system was not designed to *promote* self-interest but to check it. Self-interest is a fact that cannot be ignored. And it is an inherently ambiguous fact.

Three Types of Self-Interest

It is useful to distinguish three types of self-interest: evil, neutral, and good. Self-interest is not always expressive of evil. Some self-interests are good. A person's interest in becoming holy is not an evil interest: "What does it profit a man if he gain the whole world, and suffers the loss of his soul?" A person's interest in developing his or her own talents is not an evil interest. A person's self-interest in developing self-mastery and self-control—that is, in becoming a truly free person—is not an evil interest.

Of course, some forms of self-interest *are* evil. To seek solely one's own advantage to the unfair disadvantage of others is an evil form of self-interest. To be merely acquisitive or greedy is an evil self-interest.

Other forms of self-interest, of course, are neither clearly good nor clearly bad. Much depends upon how those interests are deployed. To seek an education, for example, may be an interest good in itself; in another sense, though, it can be neutral. A good education can be put to evil purposes as well as good purposes. As Aristotle has remarked, a clever person is sometimes capable of greater evil than one who is not so clever.

Indeed Tocqueville was quite surprised when he visited America forty years after the Constitution was adopted to find that Americans quite often used the word "self-interest" in a way he had never heard in France. In France, the term almost always denoted something negative, a kind of vice. In the United States, however, Americans described even generous and public-spirited activities as forms of self-interest. They said "self-interest" where obviously they meant "public interest." How could this be? Tocqueville explained it by the fact that Americans had come to realize that, given a beneficent system, to serve the public interest was to serve their own long-range interests and to serve their own self-interests required them to serve the public interest.

Many of the first American immigrants had labored harder and longer in Europe than here in America, where they reaped more while working less. This increase in benefits, then, could not be ascribed solely to their own efforts; the increase was given by the more favorable system. They had reason, therefore, to be grateful for the system because it served their own interests. It was in their own interest then to help the system prosper and grow. For the first time in history, self-interest and the public interest would often coincide.

What most fascinated Tocqueville, then, was the difference between the new social experiment in the United States and the older social experiments in Europe, like the Holy Roman Empire and its subsequent forms. This difference had as its fulcrum a different understanding of the relation between self-interest and the public good. This is why the Latin American priests who visited an American university for a seminar on economics understood this term self-interest in one way, whereas the North Americans with whom they studied understood it in quite another. But the difference between these two understandings needs to be brought to light.

When persons formed by a traditional Catholic society hear the word self-interest, they understand it as signifying individualism and materialism: selfishness, egoism, and possessiveness. This is not the way a society based upon ordered liberty understood the term. Indeed, Tocqueville devoted two chapters to the elucidation of the *new* meaning given to the term self-interest in the new social order. He called it "self-interest rightly understood" (See *Democracy in America* Volume II, Book 2, chapters 8 and 9). In the societies whose cultures were formed by the Holy Roman Empire, such as France, self-interest played one social function and had one form; in societies of the new order—in democracy, as Tocqueville called it, naming both the polity and the economy—self-interest had both a different practice and a different social role.

The Aim of the New Order

In the New World, citizens were engaged in building new communities—indeed, in *constituting* new communities of a new type. That their main interest was communitarian went without saying. The framers of the U.S. Constitution were quite explicit:

> We the People of the United States, in Order to form a more perfect Union, establish Justice, insure domestic Tranquility, provide for the common defence, promote the general Welfare, and secure the Blessings of Liberty to ourselves and our Posterity, do ordain and establish this Constitution for the United States of America.[6]

They spoke explicitly of constituting a new order. This was analogous to that full "Reconstruction of the Social Order" that Pope Leo XIII was to call for universally in *Rerum Novarum* in 1891.

The aim of the new order was to build a system both of incentives for creative, society-building actions and of checks and balances against negative, merely self-seeking, anarchic, and socially destructive actions. The framers were designing a new order for sinners, after all, and for citizens born not yet free, not yet masters of themselves, not yet persons of virtue but only striving to become so, in order to live as worthy of their God-given destiny as free men and women. Liberty, Tocqueville often remarked, is a long schooling in virtue.[7] It is not easy for humans to master their passions, their prejudices, and their ignorance so as to be able to live as free men and women. In addition, they need to learn how to live in a cooperative, socially creative, and inventive society. For human beings do not live alone, self-sufficient as angels. To live together in a free society, humans require a high degree of social virtue.

Thus, the problem for all those who seek the liberation of the human race from torture and from tyranny, from poverty and misery, and from the virtually universal oppression of conscience, information, and ideas is twofold: to confront the fact of existing sinful structures, and to construct incentives, checks and balances so that from sin "structures of virtue" might emerge. In short, as the theologians say, "sinful structures" must yield to what might be called "structures of virtue." This is a long task, never completed. Thus, in illustrating the pictorial shape of their *Novus Ordo*, the framers chose the three-sided image of a pyramid—one point each for polity and for economy at its base and the topmost point for an overarching image of religion, conscience, and morality. And they deliberately pictured this pyramid as *incomplete*, signifying that *liberty* and *justice* are goals so transcendent that the human race is ever advancing toward them but never fully and finally achieves them. No human society ever attains the fullness of the Kingdom of God on earth. All remain sinful. All remain under the all-knowing judgment of the unblinking eye of the Almighty.

Capitalism and "Caput"

Like the term self-interest, so the word capitalism has a different meaning in different cultures. Pope John Paul II captures the true meaning perfectly in his encyclical *Sollicitudo Rei Socialis* (1987), when he speaks of the inalienable "right to personal economic initiative," endowed in every single human being by the Creator.[8] The Creator has formed every human being in His own image. Every Jew, every Christian, indeed every human being has an inalienable vocation to become creative. This gift is given to every human being not solely for herself or for himself, the pope points out, but for "the common good." In this gift is the germ of human development. A newborn child is not solely an open mouth, intended to consume, but a brain, a heart—a being able to create within his or her lifetime far more than he or she consumes. This endowment is the very basis of human development. Without it, human beings could not be creative, could not invent, could not bring about development.

What is a capitalist system, in its true meaning? It is a system of institutions designed to liberate the creativity of the human mind. It is the mind-centered system. Thus its name: from the Latin *caput*, "head" or "mind." Thus, Max Weber speaks of the *spirit* of capitalism. Capitalism is a new order in history precisely because it is centered more than any other system on the creativity of the human mind. Therein lies its historical fertility.

Capital does not consist only in things, material goods, instruments of production. During World War II, the entire material "capital" base of Germany and Japan, for example, lay in devastation and ruins. Yet the wealth of those nations lay not primarily in material things but in the creative minds of their citizens, in indestructible qualities of the human spirit. From this source, as from a well, the economic miracles of the postwar world sprang.

As we have seen, capitalism does not consist solely in private property, markets, or profits. Traditional, precapitalist societies had all these. What was specifically new about the new order that arose toward the end of the eighteenth century was its original, history-making emphasis upon "intellectual property": upon the insight that the cause of the wealth of nations is not labor but mind, upon the protection (for a time and for the sake of a dynamic common good) of patents and copyrights.[9] The wealth of the developed nations is in every case rooted in the liberation of the creative minds of all their citizens.[10]

In this sense, the "structures of virtue" most necessary for the liberation of the poor from poverty and misery are institutions that enable all citizens, especially the poor, to exercise their God-given "right to personal economic initiative," to become in fact what they have been created to become, namely, creative. When every citizen creates more than he or she consumes, then development occurs. Human creativity is the central dynamic of history. That is why Pope John Paul II is especially prescient in seeing that the fundamental line of human history begins at the beginning, in the story of creation. The main story of the human race is the story of liberty.[11]

God did not make the nations equal in their endowments or natural resources. As Cardinal Hoeffner noted, God's purpose in making the nations diverse and unequal was so that each of them would be obliged to make up for its own lacks by trading with others.[12] God willed that all members of His family would live in mutual interdependence. Each would have needs that could only be supplied by others. Indeed, the Spanish Jesuits of Salamanca were among the first scholars of the world to grasp the role of commerce and trade in bringing about an interdependent world, based upon law and consent.[13] (One does not have to be Protestant to grasp the "spirit of capitalism," or the "right to personal economic initiative." These are human, natural rights, belonging to all persons universally.)

In brief, without "structures of virtue," neither genuine democracy nor a developing economy can be made to work. Human capacities for creativity, for cooperation, and for seeking the common good must be undergirded by social incentives. Still, the existing foundation on which structures of virtue must be built is sinful structures. Thus, human capacities for sin, selfishness, and social destructiveness must be countered and blocked by checks and balances, fruitfully and effectively constructed.

No liberation can succeed that is not solidified in practical institutions. No liberating institutions can be made to work without the practice of basic human virtues, both social and personal. Thus, the task of social reconstruction begins with a careful analysis of human sinfulness. It proceeds through the long schooling in virtue that prepares men and women to live as free citizens ought to live, in institutions that nourish creativity.

The Universal Vocation

Today, the Catholic church—indeed, the whole of humanity—is committed to liberating the poor from tyranny and torture, through democracy; from poverty, through a creative economy based upon the right to personal economic initiative; and from the oppression of conscience, ideas, and information, through a free and open culture. These three liberties belong together: political, economic, and moral-cultural. Each is a necessary but not sufficient condition for the other two.

Today, every true democracy on this planet has as its economic base a capitalist economy. Empirically, capitalism is a necessary but not sufficient condition for democracy.[14] A capitalist economy leads to an ever-larger middle class, ever more highly educated, that soon demands self-government and resists rule by the military. In practice, the free economy typically comes first.

Democracy then typically rises from this base. Beyond the creative economy, such nations as Singapore, South Korea, and Chile teach us that without democracy, a free economy is vulnerable, not least in securing political legitimacy and during transitions of power. Thus, democracy is a necessary but not a sufficient condition for the long-term stability of capitalism. Capitalism without democracy is vulnerable to being swiftly abandoned. A mind-centered economy and an expanded middle class press steadily toward democracy.

The purpose of a free and creative political economy is to liberate the human spirit to be itself: that is, to free the human spirit for holiness, for religious growth, for the exploration of the heights and the depths of artistic experience, and for the development of the sciences. Humans do not live by bread alone. Human liberty is not an end only. It is a means to higher achievement. How dreadful it would be to have full liberty and to use it for nothing.

The purpose of democratic capitalism as a system is *not* self-contained. Such a system, rooted in the depths of human personality and designed to express human liberty and creativity, rises to the transcendent.

Human liberty and human creativity are participations in the eternal life of God. Whoever lives the life of liberty and creativity—with its attendant risks, ambiguities, and uncertainties—receives many intimations of the divine, hears "rumors of angels."

Human beings are by nature free and creative. They were made so by their Creator. There are no such things as "American rights," or "Chilean rights," or "Japanese rights"; there are only human rights, endowed in every human being by their Creator.

Every Jew, every Christian, every human being without exception was made by God to be creative. The vocation of each of us is to create in our lifetimes a better inheritance for our children's generation than we received for ourselves. Our vocation is to create a world in which poverty no longer imprisons anyone—in which all of the poor escape from poverty.

This can be done only through universal economic activism, through universal economic creativity. During our generation, some of the peoples of Southeast Asia have proved this conclusively. The poor are more intelligent than the sophisticated sometimes think. The poor are endowed by God with a creative spark, with an instinct for personal economic initiative, with a desire to improve their own condition and to make life better for their children than it was for themselves. God Himself has made the poor creative.

Our task is to ignite, sustain, and support the creativity with which God has endowed the poor, through constructing a system of politics, economics, and morals worthy of the people God made to be free.

To liberate the poor from poverty is to build such a system. For such a task, all hands are needed. A system of natural liberty and natural creativity is the work of cooperation, the universal vocation.

6
Economic Development from the Bottom Up

Many Europeans believe that the roots of America lie in Europe. The Latin American historian German Arciniegas has taught us, however, that the opposite is true: the roots of Europe lie in America. This hemisphere, not Europe, pioneered the paths of democracy based on constitutional government and a bill of rights. This hemisphere, not Europe, pioneered economic development deriving from creativity, discovery, invention, and the broadest possible distribution of private property. In short, it was this hemisphere that taught Europe the most liberating form of political economy so far experienced in human history, that combination of democracy and capitalism that has given the peoples of the North Atlantic their freest and most prosperous forty years ever. According to Arciniegas, the Western Hemisphere—this hemisphere of liberty—has been the pioneering hemisphere.

Nonetheless, the task of human liberation, begun in this hemisphere, is far from finished. We have an immense amount yet to do—especially with regard to economic systems. Most thinkers from all points of view assert that economic poverty is the greatest impediment to liberty still remaining in our hemisphere. Although there are still political dictatorships in this hemisphere, a few years ago one could count them on one hand: Paraguay and Cuba, Chile and Nicaragua; by 1990 these were down to Cuba. Compared with practices in Africa, Asia, Europe, and the Middle East, *political* liberty is far advanced in North America and South America. The *economic* desperation of some 200 million persons in Latin America, however, remains an outrage to our consciences.

Central and South America are rich in natural resources, far richer than Japan, South Korea, Taiwan, Hong Kong, and Singapore. Compared with other regions of the world, Latin America is very rich in natural resources, but its economic systems have not been designed to use those resources creatively. The poverty of millions in Latin America is painful precisely because it is so unnecessary.

What Is the Nature of Wealth?

What are the nature and the cause of the wealth of nations? The natural resources of the tiny islands that constitute Japan are few, but Japan is one of the wealthiest of nations. The natural resources of Brazil are immense, but many Brazilians are desperately poor. The springs of wealth do not lie primarily in natural resources: the original form of wealth is not material; the original form of wealth lies in the human mind, in human culture and habits.

In *Laborem Exercens*, Pope John Paul II uses the word capital to denote inanimate objects such as money and machines. This usage is quite common but does not quite go to the root of the matter. The original form of capital is human capital. After the terrible destruction wrought in Western Europe by World War II, the material capital of Europe lay in rubble. But the human capital that remained in the minds and habits of the European people became the source of the "European miracle." For this miracle, human capital had only to be matched to a form of political economy that liberated it. The cause of the wealth of nations is the dynamic image the Creator placed in every human mind and heart. The purpose of a liberating political economy is to allow this mustard seed of creativity to grow to its full stature.

Every human being is born to be a creator. During a lifetime each is able to create far more than he or she consumes. When in any nation the aggregate of individual creativity is greater than the aggregate of individual consumption, the wealth of that nation increases. The cause of the wealth of nations is human creativity.

Thus, to understand contemporary economic life, one must place far more emphasis upon spiritual factors than upon material ones, since material resources are apparently becoming less and less important in our world. Nations whose wealth springs from the human spirit stand among the wealthiest and are growing most rapidly. Those whose wealth comes primarily from natural resources find that market prices of raw materials are declining, since the world apparently needs such resources less and since, in their place, new materials are constantly being produced. Thus, the incredibly powerful silicon chips used in computers are made from humble and plentiful sand. Prices for raw materials such as copper have been experiencing a long, slow slide. Fiber optics are replacing copper. By an intellectual route different from what is usually followed, then, we come to a central point: of all the resources available to any nation, its material resources are less important than the minds and habits of its citizens. The sources of creativity lie in the spirit of invention, discipline, and order. In economics, too, the primacy of spirit is vindicated.

Thus I come to my major thesis: those who wish to liberate human beings from poverty within their nation should look to its primary resource, the minds and spirits of the citizens *at the bottom* of society. The cause of the wealth of nations is the empowerment of such persons. To empower people is the indispensable first step toward rapid economic development.

Rapid economic development has already happened in several nations in less than twenty years. Photographs of South Korea, Taiwan, Singapore, Hong Kong, and other nations of the Southeast Asian rim in 1945, or even in 1965, and statistical profiles of those countries then compare interestingly with those of today. In 1966, the per capita income of South Korea was $125, and in 1986 it reached $2,250. These countries have virtually eliminated the misery and dire poverty that characterized them only twenty years ago. Since poverty is a relative concept, parts of their populations remain poor, but the poverty of today is no longer the bitter and desperate poverty of twenty years ago. The first point then is that rapid economic development can take place with surprising speed; in several places, it has.

The second point is that rapid economic development is a matter of *system*. Everywhere on earth human beings are capable of creativity. But the systems that liberate that creativity are not so universal. Whether a system of political economy liberates human creativity or inhibits it is the crucial factor. Does a system of political economy enhance the creative economic virtues of its citizens, or does it penalize them? This is the critical question for development. If we wish to build up the virtues of the citizenry, Aristotle tells us, we must look to the ethos of the *polity*: that is, look to system. In some ways, the system counts more than individuals. In other ways, the reverse is true. Individual human beings are free to question, to criticize, and to change the systems of political economy under which they live; hence the actions of individual citizens are not fully determined by the nature of the systems. Citizens transcend systems.

Nonetheless, the weight of a system upon individuals is very heavy indeed. Consider noble citizens in a Latin American country suffering from an inflation rate of more than 100 percent a month. Suppose that those citizens have saved the equivalent of $14,000 for the education of their children. As virtuous citizens, these parents would prefer to invest that money in their homeland, so that the internal capital of the nation grows and so that such investments will nourish further growth. But if they do invest at home, the value of their savings will be eroded by the rate of inflation and will soon be worth very little. If they do not invest this money at home but instead invest it abroad, how then will their country ever develop? It will suffer from severe capital flight. In this way and in many others, a system can frustrate even citizens of outstanding human virtue.

The central question for political economy, therefore, becomes this: How do we construct institutions—how do we construct a system—that is worthy of the creativity with which God has endowed every single person? It is not easy to design a system of political economy worthy of its citizens, if these citizens are as they are described in the Jewish and Christian testaments: free in intellect and will and drawn to imitate God in creativity, in truth, in justice, and in love. It is not easy to bend the poor materials of politics and economics into such a shape as to make them worthy of such citizens. Nonetheless, that is the task that the founders of the various nations of the New World set for themselves, as they have tried for two centuries to create in this hemisphere a *novus ordo seclorum*.

Creativity Requires Property

Because the source of creativity lies in each single human person, one must design a political economy that reaches all citizens universally, from the bottom up. One must try to protect and to nurture the liberty of each person, without exception. One must design social institutions that liberate the virtues of citizens at the grass roots.

Moreover, because every human person is an incarnate spirit, composed of body and soul, the human spirit must be capable of expressing itself in the material world, if human liberty is to be efficacious in history. From this insight, Thomas Aquinas drew the necessity of private property.[1] Without property under the dominion of every citizen, that citizen's liberty of action is curtailed. But private property is also an incentive reaching across the generations, encouraging every human being to work not only for himself or herself but also for their loved ones down the ages. A further reason for preferring a regime of private property, then, is that as a social system it serves the common good better than any other. Many centuries ago, St. Bernardine explained this point through a story:

> Have you heard the story about the donkey of the three villages? It happened in the Valley of the Moon. There was a large shed close to the windmill. In order to take the grain to the mill, three villages agreed to buy a donkey and keep him in the shed.
> A dweller of the first town went for the donkey, took him to his home, loaded the animal's back with a heavy bag of wheat, and led him to the mill. During the milling, he released the ass so he could graze, but the fields had become barren because of heavy treading. When the wheat was

milled, he collected the flour, loaded it on the donkey, and returned home. The man unloaded the ass and brought him to the shed, muttering to himself, "He who used him yesterday must have given him a lot of grass. Surely, he is in no need now," and left the donkey.

The following day, a villager from the second town went for the donkey. He took him to his farm, placed on him a heavier burden than the day before, and—without feeding him—led the animal to the mill. With the milling over and the flour already at home, the villager returned the donkey to the shed thinking that yesterday's user must have treated the animal well. And, yes, he left the donkey saying, "Oh, I am very busy today." Two days had passed, and the donkey still did not have a bite.

On the third day, someone from the third village arrived for the donkey and burdened him with the heaviest load yet. "This donkey is owned by the Municipality," he remarked, "so it must be strong." And he took him to the mill. But on the way back, with the wheat already milled, the donkey was sluggish and often halting. The villager had to whip him, and after a strenuous effort, they arrived at the shed. The villager complained, "What an ass this Municipality bought to serve three towns! He is a piece of trash!" That day also the donkey was not fed.

Do you want to know how it ended? The fourth day, the poor beast collapsed and was torn to bits.[2]

As this story from St. Bernardine shows, even the precapitalist traditional society had learned by experience that a regime of private property serves the common good better than a regime of collective ownership. That is why most traditional, precapitalist societies preferred regimes of private property, markets, and incentives. These techniques do not constitute capitalism: they are traditional and precapitalist. A genuinely capitalist society is not born until a further insight is grasped and society is organized around it: the cause of the wealth of nations is mind. Therefore, institutions favorable to invention, discovery, the spread of universal education, and the liberation of the practical intellect of individuals are necessary.

This was the reason why, in the United States, Abraham Lincoln was so determined to open the West through a crucial action of the state, the passage of the Homestead Act. Lincoln did not want the United States to be built according to the social system of the American South, which consisted of many large plantations. Lincoln wanted the rest of the United States opened up on the principle of free labor, not slave labor. His idea was that it is out of liberty that enterprise springs:

> Without the *Constitution* and the *Union,* we could not have
> attained the result; but even these, are not the primary cause
> of our great prosperity. There is something back of these,
> entwining itself more closely about the human heart. That
> something, is the principle of "Liberty to all"—the principle
> that clears the *path* for all—gives *hope* to all—and, by conse-
> quence, *enterprize,* and *industry* to all.[3]

Free labor would lead to broad upward mobility throughout society
and also to much greater prosperity through the use of the applied
intelligence of every single individual to the immediate problems at
hand.[4] A hundred thousand independent farmers have more social
intelligence than do a small collective band of state authorities at-
tempting to plan an economy. This was the hypothesis, the experiment. From this experiment grew the wealth of the United States.[5]

Human creativity requires property ownership by individuals.
To maximize human creativity, one must maximize private ownership:

> For the mass of men the idea of artistic creation can only be
> expressed by an idea unpopular in present discussions—the
> idea of property. The average man cannot cut clay into the
> shape of a man; but he can cut earth into the shape of a
> garden; and though he arranges it with red geraniums and
> blue potatoes in alternate straight lines, he is still an artist;
> because he has chosen. The average man cannot paint the
> sunset whose colours he admires; but he can paint his own
> house with what colour he chooses; and though he paints it
> pea green with pink spots, he is still an artist; because that
> is his choice. Property is merely the art of the democracy. It
> means that every man should have something that he can
> shape in his own image, as he is shaped in the image of
> Heaven.[6]

One must do this at the bottom of society. As an ideal, the good
society should seek universal property ownership. This ownership
should not necessarily be in land. It may be in broadly distributed
private ownership of the means of production, as for example in the
workers' share of ownership in the companies for which they work,
the ownership by workers of pension plans, and the like.

But there is also property in mind.[7] One of the most important
steps taken by the framers of the system of political economy in the
United States is found in Article 1, Section 8, no. 8, of the Constitution:

> The Congress shall have the power . . . to promote the
> progress of science and useful arts, by securing for limited

times to authors and inventors the exclusive right to their respective writings and discoveries.

Here an important insight is incorporated into public law. A crucial form of property is ownership of ideas; and ideas are at the very heart of creativity. Meanwhile, experience shows that creative persons such as authors and inventors are stimulated by incentives, particularly the incentive of owning for a time the fruits of their own discoveries. Of course, if these ideas do not serve the common good and go unappreciated by the people, these ideas do not bear immediate fruits. But if they do serve the common good, then authors and inventors should share in these fruits. By this means, an immense tide of invention and discovery was unleashed in a systematic, socially contrived way for the first time in human history.

Philosophically and theologically, a regime emphasizing the broadest possible distribution of private property empowers citizens to act in the world of material things through material instruments of their own. But whether a regime of private property actually achieves a higher level of the common good than any other system is not a philosophical or theological matter: it is an empirical matter.

The main historical rivals to a regime of private property have been two: the tribalism that Julius Caesar described among the Germanic tribes in ancient times and the ideological socialism of the nineteenth century. Empirically, tribal collectivism was unable to attain as high a level of the common good as regimes of private property did. Thus, they began to disappear from history. Empirically, much the same appears to be happening to the Socialist regimes extant today. Socialist regimes are doomed by human nature.

Nonetheless, the problem before us is not ideological. While it is a question of system and therefore requires theory, the problem itself is practical: how to help the poor of Latin America to be poor no longer. This could be achieved by the year 2000, or not much beyond it, if we were to secure the right social changes. As the populations of the Asian rim have proved, so much success can be registered in such a very short time. Beginning from a lower economic base and possessing fewer natural resources, they nonetheless succeeded. And so can Latin Americans.

What Should Be Done?

Among the most important things to do are the following:

• Maximize popular ownership, especially home ownership, the ownership of small businesses, workers' shares in commerical or agricultural corporations, and the like.

• Change legal structures so that the incorporation of small businesses becomes cheap (no more than a day's wage), easy (only one registrar of incorporation papers to deal with), and quick (requiring no more than the exchange of papers of request and approval through the mail, about two weeks). The state does not create corporations; citizens do through their voluntary consent. The state merely records duly prepared incorporation papers.

• Change laws and restructure banking institutions so that credit becomes universally available to poor persons. The poor need credit to acquire property, to create and improve small businesses, to finance their further education, and otherwise to expand the range of their economic activities.

• Change laws to protect patents and copyrights to spur the creativity and inventiveness throughout the population. Given opportunity, the most talented among the poor swiftly become the most creative segment of society.

• Encourage the development of private school systems, particularly secondary schools and universities. And encourage links between education and the practical arts and sciences necessary for economic development.

• Concentrate large private and public investment in universal education. And link universal education to increased economic productivity in every sector of society. The human capital developed through education is the chief cause of the wealth of nations.

All these recommendations spring from one central core. The cause of the wealth of nations lies within citizens themselves, in their native capacities for creativity, in their propensities for improving their condition, and in the insights, habits, and skills they acquire as they prepare themselves for economic activism. The liberty and responsibility of individual citizens are a nation's priceless asset: these must be nourished, enlarged, sustained.

It is important for economic development to proceed universally, without leaving anybody out. Every person has obligations to the common good; the common good is enhanced by the efforts and successes of every individual. Society as a whole needs the eager hands and alert minds of all its citizens. Care should therefore be taken to make sure that all are prepared to become economic activists.

Again, incentives open to all must be set in place. Empirically, appealing to individuals to become economically active for the sake of the common good does not seem to do much good. They are more likely to become economically active if they see that through their labor they will be able to improve their own condition and that of their families. Their motive for becoming economically active is less important for the common good than the fact that they become economically active. God will be the judge of their motives; from the point of view of public policy, it suffices that citizens cooperate industriously and creatively with their fellows, in contributing to the activities that constitute a dynamic and growing economy.

It is important to note, too, that economic activism is not morally neutral. To act in an economically fruitful and creative way, citizens must have already mastered certain virtues. These virtues are the *sine qua non* of a developing economy. Economic growth arises only when citizens are willing to postpone the satisfactions of today to attain the growth of tomorrow. Thus, spirit must triumph over flesh, the future over the present, delayed return over current pleasure.

To achieve this result, societies must provide a secure structure of custom and law. If no one can trust the future, or if no clear path leads between today and tomorrow, many will think it foolish to give up the bird in their hand for two in the bush.

A tradition of fairness is both a necessary condition for stable social expectations and an immense spiritual acquisition. Only when people believe the law to be fair will they respect the law. Only then can their stable expectations thrive. Economic growth is a fruit of the human spirit. There are no shortcuts to it; those who take shortcuts pay a long-term price. (Thus, those Middle Eastern nations that have benefited from the easy money that flows from oil will suffer a grievous penalty when the oil runs out, if they have invested too little in developing the economic habits, skills, and attitudes that generate the true wealth of nations.) The Japanese have almost no natural resources; their wealth springs from hardiness and creativity of spirit.

Political Economy in Latin America Today

The political economy of Latin America today is still in embryo, nourished from many different roots. In large tracts throughout Latin America, one still encounters a rudimentary barter economy, hardly changed from the tribal customs of the Indians. To an outsider, though, the most impressive feature of Latin American economies is their degree of state control and the spirit of patrimonialism and mercantilism that they inherited from fifteenth-century Spain and Portugal. In some sectors, social democratic traditions, particularly from southern Europe, have shaped thinking. Meanwhile, in the bookstores of the universities, one sees stacks filled with what Raymond Aron once referred to as "the Marxist Vulgate." These universities, of course, are predominantly sponsored by the state, and their graduates are most likely to become functionaries of the state, in one form or another: in schools, hospitals, study centers, and research institutes as administrators, social workers, meteorological experts, engineers, and so on.

As a sort of thought experiment, one can ask oneself, How much more of Latin American life would come under state control if its economic systems became directly Socialist? Even today, most of the economy in most Latin American nations is in the hands of the state. The scope for imagination, creativity, and initiative of millions of citizens in Latin America is very narrow indeed.

Nonetheless, as Hernando de Soto has shown, most of the poor in Latin America today are not industrial workers or even employed by others. A large majority of the poor are entrepreneurs.[8] They make artifacts and try to market them, or provide services. Without the power to incorporate themselves, without access to credit, without insurance, these "informals" show all the "propensities to truck and barter" found universally. Although the human race is enterprising, the legal structures of traditionalist, precapitalist societies obstruct and frustrate the native instincts of their active citizens. This is a form of economic suicide, a kind of abortion of the primary source of national economic development. The bread of honest enterprise is snatched from the mouths of citizens; the fruit of their minds and hands is crushed underfoot. "The sum of good government," Thomas Jefferson warned his fellow citizens in his first inaugural in 1800, is "a wise and frugal government, which shall restrain men from injuring one another, which shall leave them otherwise free to regulate their own pursuits of industry and improvement, and shall not take from the mouth of labor the bread it has earned."

In all of Latin America today, there are some 70 million youngsters, already born, under the age of fifteen. During every year between now and the year 2005, these young people will be seeking employment as they come of age. Where will the jobs for them be found?

Only a small proportion of Latin Americans can be engaged in agriculture, which is becoming more efficient and less labor intensive with every passing year. Large manufacturing establishments seem unlikely to multiply rapidly, although some growth will doubtless be experienced. The key to the future of Latin America lies, then, in one place only: the most rapid possible growth in the small business sector. The facilitation of local enterprise—both in manufacturing and in services—will be as fundamental to economic development in Latin America as it has been in other economically successful nations.

Enterprise works best from the bottom up. Enterprise must have the widest possible popular base. The wealth of nations does not trickle down from the top: it wells up from the bottom. The habits of enterprise are evident among the poor of Latin America. Matched to a system that respects and nourishes them, such habits will lift the poor out of poverty. That is the only preferential option for the poor worthy of free men and women: namely, that the poor should no longer be poor, but on the contrary, economically successful, masters of their own economic destiny. Nothing strengthens democracy more than a broad, dynamic, universally enjoyed economic growth, which allows individuals to rise as high as their talents take them.

The error Marxists make is nostalgia for a nineteenth-century theory, a false one at that, which holds that labor is the source of value. Mind is the source of value and the primary cause of economic development. The error Socialists make is to hold that poverty can be overcome by redistributing current wealth, rather than by creating abundant new wealth. This is why existing Socialist societies are empirically so stagnant, gray, and deadening. (A further error is to give equality primacy over liberty and thus to strengthen the power of the administrative state.) The error Christian Democrats make is to emphasize democracy without grasping its precondition: a dynamic, growing economy that allows the poor to better their condition.

The key to economic development is moral. "The revolution is moral or not at all," Charles Peguy used to say. The polity and the economy must be shaped to nourish the virtues of political citizenship and economic activism. Thus, a humane social revolution requires three liberations: liberation from torture, tyranny, and lawlessness through democracy and institutions of human rights; liberation from poverty through institutions favorable to the creativity of all citizens, especially the poorest; and the liberation of moral energies through the inculcation of the virtues of law-abidingness, fairness, cooperation, creativity, and enterprise—under institutions that free conscience, information, and cultural life from tyrannical repression.

"The God who made us, made us free," Thomas Jefferson wrote. In human freedom—the great legacy of Jewish and Christian wisdom—lies the creativity through which men and women fulfill their vocations to become what God made them to be: images of Himself.

Addendum

Experience in Latin America teaches me that some will raise questions about the "debt crisis." I would like to make a few points.

1. South Korea has one of the largest external debts of any nation, especially for a nation of its size (a population of 43 million); its debt is $46.7 billion. South Korea uses the principal it has borrowed so creatively, however, that its borrowing precipitates no "crisis." On the contrary, South Korea uses what it borrows to make a profit. It pays its interest on time. It pays back the principal on a routine basis, as scheduled. Korea

proves that borrowing capital can be a great boon to a nation prepared to invest that capital fruitfully.

2. Even worse than the debt crisis is the massive "capital flight" of economic gains reaped by Latin Americans but invested abroad. Since broad economic growth depends on indigenous local investment, such capital flight suggests a lack of confidence in the structures of Latin American law and government policies. Policies, for example, that fail to control inflation—that lead too quickly to "printing money"—cause a breakdown in confidence.

3. Government tax policies need also to be examined. As a general rule, high tax rates bring in low aggregate revenues, whereas reasonably low rates bring in high aggregate revenues. (This occurs because high rates stimulate tax evasion and capital consumption rather than productive investment.) Tax policy should be subjected to intense moral scrutiny, so that it achieves the best possible practical effects. The aim of government policy should be to encourage creative investment that spurs broad economic growth, taxed at rates likely to bring in maximum actual revenues. These two goals—creative economic growth and high actual revenues—are best fulfilled at a calculable rate, based upon national and international experience.

4. New U.S. lending and investment of capital in Latin America have fallen off dramatically since 1985. This drop in U.S. lending and investment, in the face of large capital outflows from Latin America to pay interest on earlier debts and also in the face of the continuing flight of indigenous capital, has meant net capital outflows from some Latin American nations. This is tragic.

5. The Vatican statement recommending face-to-face dialogue between debtors and creditors provides a sound basis for resolving the continuing Latin American debt crisis in a step-by-step, practical, innovative way. The Vatican's emphasis upon structural reforms within the debtors' political economies, to enhance steady economic growth, would be proper even without a debt crisis. Its argument that creditors should further seek to renegotiate, to convert, or to write down debts is also cogent. This process is well under way.

6. A most promising development appears to be the conversion of debts, at discounted values, into shares of ownership of the debt-bearing assets. The creditors accept a write-down. In return, the written-down amounts of debt are converted into partial ownership of the indebted enterprises. Such devices lighten the immediate financial burdens on the ledgers both of borrowers and of lenders. They also involve both in the mutual interests inherent in partnership.

7. The waters to be navigated by such transactions are uncharted; innovative solutions must be weighed, experimented with, and winnowed.

8. Three aims should guide such renegotiations: the restructuring of Latin American economic systems in ways that will promote the broad economic growth beneficial to their societies; second, the opening of Latin American economies to the economic activism of the "informals"

and others among the poorest, so that those at the bottom can help both to produce economic growth and to enjoy its benefits; and, third, the resumption of net capital inflows from North America, Japan, and Western Europe, to feed economic growth in the future.

7
Wealth and Virtue—
The Development of Christian
Economic Teaching

For many centuries, commerce and industry were looked upon as morally inferior occupations, and the desire to make money was frowned upon. Indeed, so tight was the hold of the aristocratic classes upon the imagination of moralists, as well as upon the daily lives of persons of lower station, that morality itself was described in terms of "the noble" as distinct from the merely "useful" or, still lower, "the pleasant." Nonetheless, beginning in the seventeenth and eighteenth centuries—especially in Scotland—a group of Western European moralists became skeptical of the moral biases of the aristocratic class and developed the thesis that a regime based upon commerce, and pursuing plenty as well as and even more than power, offered the most reasonable route to the moral betterment of the human race. They undertook a massive transvaluation of Western ideas of wealth and virtue. Where earlier generations found the pursuit of plenty, of wealth, and of commerce morally inferior, they found it morally superior to the foundations of any previous regime.

This "moral argument for capitalism before its triumph," as A. O. Hirschman puts it, has been too little noted—is indeed almost entirely overlooked—by moralists of our time, both religious and secular. Nonetheless, both aristocratic habits of mind and anticapitalist beliefs have led most of our fellow intellectuals to be content in this ignorance. Perhaps for vaguely "progressive" motives, they do not wish to believe that a moral case was in fact made on behalf of capitalist economies before their founding. Although the evidence of the immense benefits for prosperity, liberty, and moral progress ushered into history by capitalist economies lies before their eyes, they go on as if it does not exist.

I propose to rehearse briefly the history of this decisive transformation of morals. Other writers have stressed the dazzling successes of science, industry, medicine, and technological inventiveness that have uniquely characterized capitalist societies. But since wherever humans are both free and prosperous, and thus burdened by responsibility for making choices about what to do with their ample freedoms, moral arguments necessarily play an ever-larger role—and since ours is an age in which political illusions and excessive hopes for salvation through economic or technological successes have fallen in public repute—it is now even more important to grasp the moral basis of the historic and original argument for capitalism. Beginning with the ancient Jewish and Christian ethos regarding wealth and virtue, I then move to the revolutionary period that gradually transformed it and advanced its purposes.

The Jewish and Christian Ethos

Irving Kristol has remarked about the difference between Jewish and Christian thinking on economics that in both its prophetic and its rabbinic traditions, Jewish thought has always felt comfortable with a certain well-ordered worldliness, whereas the Christian has always felt a pull toward otherworldliness.[1] Jewish thought has had a candid orientation toward private property, commercial activity, markets, and profits, whereas Catholic thought—articulated from an early period chiefly among priests and monks—has persistently tried to direct the attention of its adherents beyond the activities and interests of this world to the next. As a result, tutored by the law and the prophets, ordinary Jews have long felt more at home in this world, while ordinary Catholics have regarded this world as a valley of temptation and as a distraction from their proper business, which is preparation for the world to come.

To be sure, the difference between the horizons within which these two major religious traditions act is mitigated by the exile and diaspora inflicted on the Jews two generations after the birth of Christ. In this respect, Jewish people too have come to regard themselves as an exiled people, who in a ceremonial way annually commemorate an inner call toward the future: "Next year in Jerusalem." In this, there is an analogy, although no more than that, between the Jewish and the Christian sense of exile. One might be tempted at first to say that the difference crucial to this analogy—for "analogy" in this sense always points to essential differences as well as to a partial similarity—is that the focus of Jewish concern for the future has a more worldly component than the Christian: the regaining of the territorial integrity of Israel, centered in Jerusalem. Yet, in Jewish experience, too, the hazards of existence demand that rest in the achievement of that aim must always be postponed into the future—in the ultimate, to the coming of the Messiah. Until then, there is always the "not yet," and there is always ahead a pilgrimage yet to make.

Rather, the essential difference seems to lie in the obligatory seriousness with which Jews must take their survival and prospering in the world, until the Messiah comes, whereas the Christian faith, accepting Jesus as the awaited Servant, Son of God, and Messiah, views this world and its striving within the horizon of a "new economy of salvation," which relativizes and diminishes the urgency of what happens "here below in this vale of tears." Once the early Christian community realized that the promised Second Coming of the Messiah was not imminent, however, and that Christians too would have to live in diaspora "until he comes again," they recognized that they required a certain worldliness—a "holy worldliness," they might hope—and a patient "building up of the Kingdom until he comes again." They would need, in short, an "incarnational" ethical strategy. Christians would have to learn to live well-ordered lives within history, much as Jews do. Both communities, each in its appropriate way, would have to "await the appointed hour."

Nevertheless, Christian thought is focused upon eschatology (that end-time of the entire world, "the last things") and eternal life (that immortal participation in God's life promised to those who "eat of this bread and drink of this cup"), in a way that divides Christian worldly interests as Jewish interests are not divided. Living within a somewhat different "horizon" from that of Jews, Christians see "the world" differently. For one thing, compared with Jews, they assign to Jesus Christ a wholly different role in world history. For Christians, it is not just that history is divided into "before Christ" and "after Christ," or that Jesus is one of humankind's notable moral teachers. Rather, Jesus Christ is Son of God and Logos, the form in whose imitation all of creation has been created, lives, and has its being. This is, admittedly, what can only be called a mystical horizon, that is, seeing that all things participate in God's life, lead to him, are—as it were—fired by him as ingots are by flame. It means seeing, in addition, that the *particular* form of human life that Jesus lived is not only a model to be imitated but the highest form in which human ethical striving, intended and graced by the Creator, can participate: suffering love, agape, that laying down one's life for others in whose light all of life has been foreseen, created, and redeemed.

Insofar, then, as they are infused with this vision and not merely baptized, Christians must see the circumstances of daily life in a unique way. They are both caught in an eschatological tow (history is not merely static but moving, developing, heading toward its fruition in full participation in the life of God) and pulled upward by a viewpoint *sub specie aeternitatis* (in the light of eternity), from whose height all worldly activities are seen to participate in the larger drama of the calling "home" of every human being, body and soul. Nonetheless, Christians are to be *in* the world, as well as *of* the world: eschatologically drawn but also incarnational. Properly seen, each human being is not a soul only, and Christianity is not a spiritualizing religion in the sense of rejecting the human body. (This is the crucial significance of the Incarnation, the Ascension, and even the Assumption into heaven of the Blessed Virgin Mary.) As the Eternal God becomes flesh and in the flesh ascends into heaven, and as the first of the redeemed, his mother, is assumed body and soul to his side, so also not only the soul but the whole human person, body and soul, is the focal point of salvation. This is also the reason for the dreadful battles of the first millennium (and more) of Christian history by the orthodox community against the body-despising gnostics, the spiritualizers, the Cathars, and others. Besides its eschatological side, Christianity also has a this-worldly, bodily, incarnational side.

In brief, it is essential to the Christian horizon that it have both an eschatological-eternal role and an incarnational role. Christian faith is meant to be lived both fully and boldly in the flesh in this world, incarnationally, and also to be lived with a sense of exile, longing, and homelessness: "We have not here a lasting home." "Our hearts are restless till they rest in Thee." Christians are properly both at home in the flesh, in this world, and in the struggles of history (to build up a kingdom of truth, justice, love, and beauty). They are also pilgrims in a diaspora, in exile, and in expectation.

A Sense of History

Meanwhile, both communities, Jewish and Christian, are religions of history. For both, the decisive encounter in the human drama is the historical, autobiographical encounter of each human with his Creator, which issues in either yes or no. The axial point of history lies in the human will. And this axial point has a social as well as a personal dimension since the Creator has entered into a social covenant with all humankind. Like Jews, Christians are first constituted as a *people,* and the individual drama of affirmation or denial takes place in this social context.

Further, the Creator is conceived of in terms of intellect and will: he is Person, Light, and Truth and Lover, Beckoner, and Promise Giver. From this vision derives the Jewish and Christian interpretation of humans as creatures of reflection and choice and the drama of human history as the history of liberty. The fulcrum of existence is seen to be intellect and will: the Creator's first and man's in imitation and response.

From this emphasis, too, comes the vision of an ideal human society as one formed through appeal to reason and to choice, through covenant and compact. From it springs, as well, the sense of history as under the light of the transcendent God, a God who is undeceivable and quite demanding.[2] From such sources appear the restless drive and social dynamism of the Jewish and Christian peoples in human history. Created in the image of their Maker, Jews and Christians have a vocation to pursue the light (to inquire), to build community (to love), and to be imaginative in changing the world (to create)—under pain of judgment.

Just the same, the Christian emphasis on both eternal life and incarnation has complicated the task of Christian ethics. What should Christians do about the world in which they find themselves? Two tendencies, both essential and yet in some considerable tension, have historically manifested themselves. First, the call to witness to what is most original to Christianity, the eschatological vision and the call to eternal life, inspired many of the saints, anchorites, and early monks to live their human lives in history as life *will* be lived when the Messiah returns.[3] They have as little to do with the tasks of this world as is commensurate with a life of union with God in prayer, contemplation, and love. They do not marry. They work as a form of prayer, for their own material sustenance and independence (or are, in part, dependent on alms). They seek "poverty in spirit," both to identify with the materially poor and to subtract themselves as much as possible from worldly concerns. They surrender their wills to God by obedience to their lawful superiors (for it is in their own wills that humans are most rich and to such wealth most attached).

The irony of monastic life is, of course, that those Christian communities that first committed themselves to such unworldly and disciplined lives, such as the Benedictine and Carthusian monks of the sixth century onward, typically reaped immense worldly success. St. Benedict (c. 480–543 A.D.), for example, has become known as "the father of modern Europe." Sprouting northward from Monte Cassino, the Benedictine monasteries taught scientific farming to the wandering tribes of France and Germany; helped villages prosper well above subsistence living; inspired the construction of great churches and libraries and centers of learning and the arts; taught a form of democratic governance (their abbots being elected by all in the community); engendered a respect for hours of the day and for appointed tasks in each; pointed toward international law and culture; pioneered in far-flung commerce and exchange; and were themselves among the first examples of independent legal "corporations" in European civilization.[4] Conceived in poverty and detachment, the monasteries and their lands often became so rich and so influential in worldly affairs that they became the envy of the covetous.

In contrast to this eschatological pole of Christianity was an equally essential incarnational pole. Christians who continued to live in the world as others live, in all the occupations of daily life, as farmers, weavers, carpenters, stonemasons, merchants, and all the other trades embodied this aspect of Christianity. For centuries, these were mainly simple folk, serfs, or peasants, who lived much as citizens of the ancient world had lived. Roads and other means of travel were few and dangerous for commerce. Worldly horizons were local. Daily living was at subsistence levels, lower in bad times, better in good, but few necessities and even fewer luxuries were available through trade. One can find many descriptions of such rural life in David Hume (1711–1776) and Adam Smith (1723–1790), since ancient and medieval forms of life persisted almost universally in Europe well into the modern period.[5] Since the teachings of Judaism and Christianity had originally been cast in the language of mainly rural peoples and of relatively small cities (hardly larger than the towns of today), these teachings made direct and simple sense to those who heard them, and prosperity made slow headway.

The Concept of Wealth

Well into the modern period, however, wealth was defined in one of two basic ways: either land (which allowed the owner to draw upon the produce of many) or gold, silver, precious stones, and other treasures.[6] Before roads and travel were safe, most Europeans were at the mercy of local agriculture, experiencing famine or plenty as the rhythms of nature dictated. Trade was relatively slight, and people could not depend upon distant sources of sustenance. The vast majority lived only at subsistence level. In these circumstances, moral judgment upon wealth was fairly direct. Economics seemed to be a zero-sum game. Apart from the fluctuations of nature, there was little except local produce to buy. Money itself—in the form of pieces of gold, silver, or other metals—was in relatively fixed supply. Industry, such as that taught by the Benedictines, and good fortune could produce new wealth through larger crops and more abundant fruits. But what could one do with these? Storage capacities were limited; spoilage was an ever-present thief.

Great landholders tended to measure their wealth, and spend their substance, by gathering retainers, raising armies, and sponsoring entertainments. The best of them, living by codes of chivalry and paternal care for their subjects, treated their dependents, including their farm laborers, fairly; the worst gouged, exploited, and repressed them. Large landholders, moreover, normally won titles of nobility for services to the greater lords of the realm, such as supplying armies, goods, taxes, and other services. Individuals were taught to respect the place and status Providence had assigned them. There was considerable social fixity, not much social mobility. For feudal landholders, the raising of armies was both useful and easy. It was useful for conquest and pillage. It was easy because most people lived long stretches of the year in indolence; they were passive because they lacked the taste for better goods or luxuries as well as the means to improve their lot. Here is how David Hume, in his historical essays, described the situation:

> It is true, the ancient armies, in time of war, subsisted much upon plunder: But did not the enemy plunder in their turn? which was a more ruinous way of levying a tax, than any other that could be devised. In short, no probable reason can be assigned for the great power of the more ancient states above the modern, but their want of commerce and luxury. Few artizans were maintained by the labour of the farmers, and therefore more soldiers might live upon it.[7]

In such a context, it was possible to regard wealth, in one respect, as a fragile gift of Providence, of whose dangers and allures Christians should be wary, entailing responsibilities of stewardship on behalf of those passed on by the hand of God into one's care. Few thought about the reconstruction of the social order. Anarchy and the widespread brigandage of the highways was so omnipresent a threat that such order as there was, necessary to sound agriculture, seemed to be the primary and indispensable achievement of civilization itself. And this civilized order was precarious. Cities were walled; palaces were fortresses.

In another respect, so much wealth—particularly of the locally unobtainable sort—was gotten through piracy and conquest that wealth was often regarded as the spoils of war and as largely ill-gotten booty. Biblical texts could easily be adduced to show that wealth is, on one hand, stolen or, on the other hand—even when it was a gift of Providence, through legitimate industry or inheritance—fraught with dangers to one's soul through sins against stewardship, through distraction, through inordinate worldly cares, or even through the awakening of ambition and covetousness.

Moreover, as money came into wider use, enabling those who had it to seek out luxuries, treasures, or those rare but highly useful goods that were locally unobtainable, a still larger scope was given to

69

vices such as avarice and ambition. Indolence, apathy, lust, and gluttony may have seemed the deadliest and most common sins in earlier days, when only local agricultural goods afforded sustenance. In later time, possibilities of conquest opened up paths to even deadlier sins such as ambition and the pride of life. Countless goods later counted ordinary were in the Middle Ages so rare that the money needed to offer in exchange for them became the focal point of desire. Slowly but increasingly, possibilities of commerce and exchange again shifted the forms of temptation—to cupidity. And the fungibility of money afforded a new translation to the medieval maxim, cited more than once in Chaucer and many other writers: "*Radix malorum cupiditas:* the love for money is the root of all evil."

In a zero-sum world, however, money acquired by one seemed to subtract from the common stock available to others. Thus, those who measured their power by the contents of their counting houses were easily tempted to become misers. What they had they hoarded. So misers were held in a special moral contempt, both because others could not share in their bounty and because of the peculiar narrowing of human attention and affections in which miserliness warps the human spirit. (David Hume offers a discussion of avarice in this sense,[8] of which novelists as late as Honoré de Balzac and even François Mauriac in France and Anton Chekhov in Russia have also offered vivid portraits.)

In sum, in the premodern world, wealth played a rather different and far simpler role than it plays today.[9] Correspondingly, the moral judgment passed on it was simpler. In the whole premodern period, throughout Christendom, illness and disease ravaged the poor. Drought, the severity of the seasons, the cycles of sterility in the soil, and many other hazards of nature brought both many prolonged periods of hardship and recurrent famines. Quite often, life offered the poor considerably less than subsistence, and the average age of mortality was quite low (estimated at about eighteen or below). For such reasons, a simple life just above a bare minimum was considered something of a blessing. Little or no thought was given to eliminating poverty or even in some systematic way to changing the conditions under which the poor lived. There was enormous misery, and great bands of beggars and the indigent wandered about, at times breaking out in wild and furious rebellions as the centuries advanced.[10] In France itself, near the end of the eighteenth century, 90 percent of the population lived on a very narrow diet, spending 80 percent of its income for bread alone.[11] Thomas Jefferson in the 1780s was appalled at the misery he witnessed as ambassador to France, and Victor Hugo as late as 1832 would describe the population as *Les Misérables.*

Nonetheless, European travelers abroad recounted the still more gruelling poverty and ignorance they encountered on continents far from Europe. Montesquieu, in effect, asked what the Christian church had done—its works of mercy aside—to alter the condition of the poor from what it had been in the time of Christ. Somewhat anachronistically, he even called the Scholastics "criminals" for their neglect of the economic transformation of the social order.[12]

Meanwhile, the few wealthy lived in conspicuous luxury at the courts of the kings; great landholders built fine estates; and the cities, although nourishing a growing class of artisans, craftsmen, and merchants, were by modern standards quite humble in circumference and population. By the end of the eighteenth century, the entire world population was estimated to number about 900 million, of whom some 180 million lived in all of Europe.[13]

In such circumstances, there was little cause to speak of the creation of wealth, for it was not clear to anyone that wealth could be created, not at least in some systematic way. A few people were born wealthy. By industriousness, a local population or an extended family might gradually—and precariously—improve their condition. By taking great risks upon the seas or overland, a few merchants engaged in transnational commerce might become wealthy.[14] On the whole, though, kingdoms tended to grow rich by extending their dominion and enlarging their tax base, while the conditions of most improved by imperceptible degrees, if at all.

Although some periods and some regions were prosperous, of course, the causes of the wealth of nations had been little glimpsed— or even inquired into. Politics was the first urgent field of inquiry, not economics. While the international horizon of Christendom and the Holy Roman Empire did enlarge the parochial and regional consciousness of individual rulers[15] and the maintenance of safe roads and protection of trading caravans were slowly increasing the intensity of trade among the nations, premodern civilizations were largely agrarian, not commercial. The Franciscans and the Dominicans in Italy and France,[16] the Jesuits of Salamanca,[17] and others began to develop a theology of the laity—and, therefore, of commerce, price, markets, and taxation. But all this must yet be accounted as premodern and precapitalist. A philosophy for a commercial civilization, let alone for an inventive, dynamic, industrial civilization, was not yet ripe for development. While such a philosophy had begun to blossom in the casuistry of the schools, neither the broad social experience nor the categories of thought that would bring it to flower yet existed.

The Modern Watershed

The glories of classical Athens appeared when Athens was only, by modern standards, a small city. Built on the economic base of slavery and on the civic consciousness of a very small class of men of property, Athens had (for its size) an incredibly large army, which under Alexander conquered a vast tract of the world east of Greece. David Hume wrote:

> Throughout all ancient history, it is observable, that the smallest republics raised and maintained greater armies, than states consisting of triple the number of inhabitants, are able to support at present. It is computed, that, in all European nations, the proportion between soldiers and people does not exceed one to a hundred. But we read, that the city of Rome alone, with its small territory, raised and maintained, in early times, ten legions against the Latins.[18]

Analogously, another humble and at first fairly poor region, Scotland, brought to flower during the eighteenth century a remarkable corps of intellectuals who revolutionized the way in which the world thought about wealth and virtue: such writers as David Hume, Francis Hutcheson, Adam Smith, and Thomas Reid. These teachers of moral philosophy had a profound interest in jurisprudence, politics, and the new science (or art) of economics. In economics, the greatest of these was Adam Smith. But Smith shared in common with his fellow Scots a vocation to educate the rising new middle class, preparing them for the world of change, of industry and commerce, and of economic growth, which he and his fellows had begun to envisage for Scotland. By the late seventeenth century, the idea of increasing wealth through conquest had already come to seem disreputable—as far too destructive—and so attention began to focus upon the only alternative. Thus, John Locke wrote:

> In a country not furnished with mines, there are but two ways of growing rich, either conquest or commerce. By the first the Romans made themselves masters of the riches of the world; but I think that, in our present circumstances, nobody is vain enough to entertain a thought of our reaping the profits of the world with our swords, and making the spoil and tribute of vanquished nations the fund for the supply of the charges of the government, with an overplus for the wants, and equally craving luxury, and vanity of the people.[19]

A century later, Scotland was far poorer than England, more rural, more agrarian. It seemed to Adam Smith wise, as it had earlier to John Locke and David Hume, to begin exchanging the old traditional ways of thinking about wealth and virtue for new ways, to the benefit of the vast poor majority. They were unwilling to accept the ancient and medieval theories of virtue (from Aristotle, Cicero, the

Schoolmen, and Pico della Mirandola), designed for a small elite whose privileges depended upon a broad base of slaves and the masses of the poor.[20] For the sake of the poor, these thinkers saw much improvement to be gained by a new sort of regime, for which a new and original approach to the virtues would be required.[21] They did not so much repeal the old table of the virtues and vices as reform and revise it, to call attention to newly recognized moral failings and fresh moral possibilities.

The New Moral Vision of Hume and Smith

Thus, the first volume in Adam Smith's intended trilogy dealt with his moral vision, *The Theory of Moral Sentiments*. In his youth, Smith studied for the Presbyterian ministry, until convinced that his true calling lay more in the secular world, in the "higgling and bargaining" of the marketplaces in the free and commercial society.[22] His fundamental moral principle was that human life is relational; moral life is best learned and practiced in community.[23] Smith prided himself on constructing homely examples, taken from ordinary life. This predilection led him to call attention to the much neglected virtue of sympathy, as the foundation of his ethical code. Smith summarized the high ideal he placed before his students as the moral crown of their future lives in a commercial society:

> And hence it is, that to feel much for others and little for ourselves, that to restrain our selfish, and to indulge our benevolent affections, constitutes the perfection of human nature; and can alone produce among mankind that harmony of sentiments and passions in which consists their whole grace and propriety. As to Love our neighbour as we love ourselves is the great law of Christianity, so it is the great precept of nature to love ourselves only as we love our neighbour, or what comes to the same thing, as our neighbour is capable of loving us.[24]

In larger terms, the achievement of David Hume, and later Adam Smith, was to turn the classic tradition on the teaching of the virtues in a new direction. For them, the classic tradition was flawed in its social assumptions. More than the classical authors had revealed, it rested on the economic basis of slavery and the continued impoverishment of the poor. It therefore abstracted too much from the life conditions of all but the civic notables, the aristocracy of honor and station, on whose shoulders few onerous obligations of work, industry, or commerce pressed, since their own economic needs were provided by others. Therefore, the moral life of the aristocracy was lived within a horizon of leisure shared by few others, and their obligations to others were guided by the fairly distant and remote star of *noblesse oblige*, far above the "higgling and bargaining" of daily life in the marketplace.

For this reason, the ancient and medieval moralists had been able to concentrate mostly on *ends*, while paying scant attention to *means*. Being of the nobility (economically), they could afford to concentrate on what is noble (morally). The task of this moral aristocracy, all other things being done for them, was to shape their moral consciousness by firm reflection on the true ends of the moral life— whether the natural life or the life of faith—to avoid squandering their freedom and ease on nonessentials. Meanwhile, all those of lower station than the nobility and the clergy (whose lives enjoyed a similar detachment) were daily involved far more in the *means* of daily life: earning a living, bringing up a family, leading (as time went on) a civic life, and forming a social world. For this reason, Hume, followed by Smith, concentrated his analysis of the moral life more on its daily necessities, on the realm of means, rather than on the realm of ends.

This move, admittedly, may be dangerous for Christian ethics, since it is essential to Christian living to keep in view the horizon of eschatology and eternal life. For a Christian, ends are extremely important, as in this answer to a famous question in the *Baltimore Catechism:*

> Why did God make me? To know Him, to love Him, and to serve Him in this world and to be happy with Him in the next.

Nonetheless, practically everyone agrees that Christian social teaching even today has so far developed too little instruction for everyday living in the "higgling and bargaining" of daily life. If Hume and Smith say too little about ends, a point on which Christian teaching has been strong, perhaps those thinkers know something about means from which Christian social thought might learn. Worth consulting, in this connection, is Alasdair MacIntyre's discussion of the moral viewpoint of Aquinas, in contrast with that of modern moralists such as John Rawls and others.[25] However that may be, Smith is preeminent in his analysis of the new moral conditions that arise from the development of a commercial society out of an agrarian society. Hume, Smith, and others make at least nine distinguishable arguments in favor of the revolutionary turn toward a capitalist economy.

First, life in the premodern rural society was circumscribed not only by poverty but also by a diminished sense of possibility for self-improvement and action. Here the Scottish intellectuals saw new moral possibilities in commerce. Hume noted, for example, that economic prosperity and the virtues of liberty go together:

> Nothing tends so much to corrupt and enervate and debase the mind as dependency and nothing gives such noble and generous notions of probity as freedom and independency. Commerce is one great preventative of this custom. The manufacturers give the poorer sort better wages than any master can afford; besides it gives the rich an opportunity of spending their fortunes with fewer servants, which they never fail of embracing. Hence it is that the common people of England who are altogether free and independent are the honestest of their rank anywhere to be met with.[26]

Second, by thus ending dependency, the rise of commerce and industry awakened the rural poor out of the slumbers of idleness. In the ancient and medieval agrarian economy, like Ireland and Scotland in the eighteenth century, Hume and Smith could see side by side the traditional rural apathy and the growing bustle and excitement of commercial living. Where manufactures and mechanical arts are not cultivated, the

> bulk of the people must apply themselves to agriculture; and if their skill and industry encrease, there must arise a great superfluity from their labour beyond what suffices to maintain them. They have no temptation, therefore, to encrease their skill and industry; since they cannot exchange that superfluity for any commodities, which may serve either to their pleasure or vanity. A habit of indolence naturally prevails. The greater part of the land lies uncultivated.[27]

The lassitude of the farm meant large numbers of men available for the call to arms and the lack of economic development in the countryside. This was the devil's bargain struck by the nobility: a large pool of labor supporting the few, in exchange for continuing poverty for the many. The factor that in the future would change this, and that was already beginning to change it, Hume and Smith saw, would be the growth of manufactures, industry, and overseas commerce. These economic activities were already introducing new goods into rural areas, awakening people to fresh possibilities, and offering them incentives for changing their ancient ways and bettering their condition:

> This perhaps is the chief advantage which arises from a commerce with strangers. It rouses men from their indolence; and presenting the gayer and more opulent part of the nation with objects of luxury, which they never before dreamed of, raises in them a desire of a more splendid way of life than what their ancestors enjoyed.[28]

So what was true of the nobility was even more true of the common people: the very possibility of bettering their condition awakened them from indolence and inspired new-found energies. The more manufacturing and commerce would grow (the supply side), the larger the expectations that people set for themselves (the demand side) would grow. Their economic activities would pick up, and economic growth would begin to rumble throughout the countryside from the bottom of society up.

The third moral advantage of the commercial society is to diminish warlikeness. Before commerce had worked its moderating influence, Adam Smith points out, such was the state of affairs that "great lords . . . [made] war continually upon one another, and very frequently upon the king; and the open country . . . [was] a scene of violence, rapine, and disorder."[29] But

> commerce and manufacture gradually introduced order and good government, and with them, the liberty and security of individuals, among the inhabitants of the country, who had before lived almost in a continual state of war with their neighbours, and of a servile dependency upon their superiors.[30]

Fourth, the practices of commerce bring peoples together in more frequent and more complex interaction. In a very simple and physical sense, when markets grow and people spend more time there, even in the primitive form of village, town, and city markets, each quarter becomes more specialized and reaches farther afield to bring in goods from around the world.

Fifth, a commercial society (if one were to develop in Scotland) would mix together the ancient social classes. It would encourage a multiplicity of voluntary associations, some of them trade based or market based, but others formed for political, civic, recreational, or religious purposes.[31] From subjects, citizens would be born—inhabitants of cities and regions with a common stake in the social progress of their region and their nation. Even the number of simple conversations would multiply: city people are talking people. Literacy and learning would flower as incentives grew for learning about the world. Indeed, the Scots, like the English, had a predisposition for conversation in taverns, pubs, and meeting halls, and clubs of many sorts had already begun to form among those interested in conversing about this or that.[32]

Thus, sixth, as market activities grew, so also did popular knowledge, skills, and specialties. Techniques improved under competition, as new products and examples of better quality in old products came to be known. Tastes expanded. Imagination was stimulated. Markets awakened a thirst for more and more exchanges of information as the existence of new products and different techniques came to be known:

> Few merchants, who possess the secret of . . . importation and exportation, make great profits; and becoming rivals in wealth to the ancient nobility, tempt other adventurers to become their rivals in commerce. Imitation soon diffuses all those arts; while domestic manufactures emulate the foreign in their improvements, and work up every home commodity to the utmost perfection of which it is susceptible.[33]

Seventh, the greater the competition, the more markets require forms of civilized behavior: patient explanation, civil manners, a willingness to be of service, and fresh attempts in closing a sale to reach satisfactory mutual consent. In this sense, wrote Adam Smith, "Commerce ought naturally to be, among nations, as among individuals, a bond of union and friendship."[34] Thus, even beyond the new information they impart about products, technical progress, and the larger world, markets also bring into common exercise an important civilizing lesson: participants in markets should be civil, reasoned, and respectful of one another's point of view. To be sure, in practice things do not always proceed so smoothly; but then, when more markets than one exist, the unsatisfied can always walk away.

Eighth, in this sort of social world, the sort made possible by the replacement of agrarian ways (with their relative isolation and taciturnity) with commercial ways (with their city bustle and rapid talk), one of the most precious, high, and rare forms of moral development would awaken: the civic need for the virtue of sympathy. Smith had a very demanding and conscience-exerting notion of what sympathy entails. We might think of it, in the present context, as a reflection in the circumstances of daily life in eighteenth-century Scotland on what the Christian tradition had long meant by charity: if we are not quite called to lay down our life for our neighbor, we are at least called to give him our full and undivided attention. Sympathy, according to Adam Smith, requires an effort of imagination greater than mere empathy (or fellow feeling, of kind for kind) and greater still than merely putting oneself in one's neighbor's shoes. Empathy is too impersonal, and merely trying to imagine how *I* would feel in the other's place is still too ego centered. Rather, true sympathy entails getting out of oneself imaginatively and actually seeing and feeling the world from a horizon not one's own, not exactly as that other person happens to be seeing it, but as an *ideal observer* from within that horizon might see it.[35] In this way, one would see the world in a way perhaps deeper than either oneself or the other had seen it before, once civil intercourse with the other had given one the precious chance to discover such a way. This is a high ideal indeed.

Ninth, sympathy is germane to the requirement that the person of commerce be more objective than others, see a little farther, and discern needs and possibilities not yet served. Yet Smith does not finally commend sympathy solely because it is useful, but rather because it is good. The ideal attracted him, and he could see that it attracted his students (and readers) as well.[36] Smith's discussion, fully understood, recalls St. Thomas's definition of love: to will the good of another. That is, to will the good of the other is not necessarily to will what the other happens to be willing at the moment, which may even be harmful or destructive. Instead, it is the good, one might say, as God or the ideal observer sees it. (This is true love, which neither deceives nor is deceived.)

Thus did the civilizing practices of markets, as they opened up many possibilities for humane development, attract the moral esteem of Hume and Smith, even in the period *before* Scotland was a highly commercial society. Hume and Smith were convinced that the commercial society represented a moral advance beyond its historical predecessors. It would inspire a new civility. It would shape a new—and superior—moral ethos. It would raise the masses of the poor out of their ancient penury, enlarge their horizons and possibilities, and, meanwhile, teach all social classes new ways of conducting themselves in social interchange.

Virtue and Passion

A reader of traditional treatises on ethics will note that Hume and Smith emphasize *sentiments* rather than *virtues,* reversing the order of the classic texts. A weakness admittedly attends this usage; one may too easily slip over into consulting unreliable, untutored, and even unworthy feelings, rather than the quiet voice of reason, duty, and responsibility. In this sense, to follow one's feelings is often no liberation, but a form of slavery. Some have tried to ascribe this penchant for sentiment among British moralists to the fact that the daily sentiments of the British people, in the eighteenth century at least, were different from those of other cultures: more commonsensical, steady, honest, and civil. Such solid characteristics, in any case, were the ones Hume and Smith relied on as sentinels over the sentiments of which they approved and which they meant to be consulted. In their defense, from the point of view of the Greek and medieval classics, it may be argued that in those passages in which he talks about education, toward the end of the *Nicomachean Ethics,* Aristotle himself seems to be making an analogous point. He writes of the blessing those children receive who have learned to feel pleasure and pain for the right things and whose feelings were already tutored in ways conducive to the right ordering inherent in practical wisdom.[37] Perhaps the British emphasis on practicality led Hume, Smith, and others to begin their ethical reflections where Aristotle leaves off, with the education of the sentiments.

But there is also a deeper reason. One of the great destroyers of societies is untamed passion. The seven deadly sins all spring from errant passion: pride, lust, envy, anger, avarice, gluttony, and sloth. Any form of society that would be virtuous must quiet these passions. It must, in short, displace them from the center of social dynamics. For in the early stages of the Italian Renaissance and later throughout Europe, local princes became locked in deadly struggles to advance their power and their fame, appealing to a new morality of power and uninhibited passion, such as Niccolo Machiavelli was both to describe and to celebrate. The law of God and the natural law as articulated by classic Roman statesmen such as Cicero gave way to the autonomy of power and passion. Indeed, the focus of the expression "natural law" shifted in Machiavelli from those activities that men ought to perform or to avoid in fulfilling the possibilities of their rational nature to those activities that advance the designs of great men seeking fame and power: from what at their best they *ought* to do to what, in fact, even at their worst they were actually doing. To be obedient to the natural law, therefore, no longer meant meeting ever-higher demands of human (and Christian) virtue but, rather, following the existing and often barbarous laws of survival and the will to power. Life came to be seen as a war, and great men were almost without exception expected to be warriors (or artists who celebrated them). Even the Vatican itself, being captured in those days by rival aristocracies of power, was too often caught up in practice with this new moral reality, as Machiavelli chronicled among the courtiers of the Papal States.

But great passions for glory, fame, power, and self-assertion proved at the same time to be immensely destructive. Moral and political anarchy spread. Moreover, religion itself, once Europe became religiously divided, became at times the motive, or at least the cover, for the ambition of princes. The ages of heroes and of grand passions erupted in generations of prolonged political and religious wars. The ethos of the natural law and God's law yielded to the ethos of unbridled passions and bore the fruit of plunder, rapine, and war.

On what basis, then, would a new morality be built? How could such passions be tamed? How could human energy be shifted toward constructive, rather than destructive, aims? This is the problem that, especially in England and Scotland, moral philosophers set out to solve.

By shifting the moral ethos from the passions of the great to the sounder sentiments of ordinary people, such writers as David Hume and Adam Smith sought to construct a new ethos for Western civilization and, indeed, the world. They did not deny the power of passions such as pride, ambition, warlikeness, and the quest for power. Rather, they attempted to provide for them a new focal point: the development of the wealth that could come from commerce and from industry. This would have the advantage, they argued, of bringing to the powerful and the passionate, and in an orderly way, the very fruits that they had been seeking through anarchic and warlike means. It would yield them an abundance and a material comfort far beyond their present rough and often harsh daily circumstances, while simultaneously energizing and empowering the large populations of the rural poor. It would require peace, rather than war, and respect for law, within whose orbit alone long-term commercial and industrial contracts could be carried out and international trade raise the standards of living of all.

In his penetrating but flawed book *The Passions and the Interests: Political Arguments for Capitalism before Its Triumph*, Albert O. Hirschman has tried to discern the lineaments of this axial shift within the European (and especially the British and French) ethos.[38] Hirschman begins by confronting a fundamental problem: How did the desire for money (*cupiditas*), hitherto considered a great sin (and even "the root of all evils"), come to be accepted in European social life as a great step forward for social morality? Hirschman argues that this transformation occurred in three steps.

The first step was the debunking of the earlier religious and philosophic tradition—the tradition of natural law—as ineffectual: that is, as unable both to describe how men actually behave and to control the destructive passions. Implicitly, this step entailed the decline of the ethos of the passions, discredited by its manifest historical destructiveness.

The second step occurred when moralists began to argue that one passion or set of passions, those concerned with money making, can be made to counter and to check the more destructive passions. "A man," Samuel Johnson, for example, came to remark, "is seldom so innocently engaged as in the getting of money." In brief, it came to be argued (by Montesquieu, for example) that commerce tames the rude and destructive passions. It teaches more humble sentiments such as those of prudence and contentment with the small but steady gains that can accrue rapidly into very great gains indeed, and for whole nations, not solely for a few aristocrats. The middle classes—the bourgeoisie, whose locus of activity was the town and city—were seen to be the carrier of new and humane possibilities, and the "heroic" aristocracy was lowered in the moral calculus.

The third step lay in supplanting, as the main term of moral analysis, the central word "passions" with the word "interests." The interests, even (in Hirschman's interpretation) the primary interest of bettering one's material condition, would bring into the passions an element of rationality and stability. Interests in this way would "tame" the passions and make them safe politically. This formulation "took the form of opposing the *interests* of men to their *passions*, and of contrasting the favorable effects that follow when men are guided by their interests with the calamitous state of affairs that prevails when men give free rein to their passions."[39]

In arguing that the concept of interest was increasingly narrowed down to purely material and economic interests, Hirschman errs, I think, by not making a sufficient distinction between the British Enlightenment and that of the continent. Unquestionably, material and economic interests came to assume a larger role in those who thought about politics. "Plenty" came to rival "power" in the objectives of political thinkers and statesmen alike in the seventeenth and eighteenth centuries,[40] and plenty was seen as a precondition of power. Thus, a decisive text for Hirschman is from Adam Smith's classic formulation of the overriding motive of man:

> An augmentation of fortune is the *means* by which the greater part of men propose and wish to better their condition. It is the *means* the most vulgar and the most obvious [emphasis added].[41]

Hirschman interprets this text as a narrowing down of the ample term interests to sheerly material purposes. Yet as Smith's text shows, and as many texts in Hume also show (not least his attack on avarice), British moralists saw the "augmentation of fortune" not as an end but as a means. They went far beyond material purposes in their conception of interests. By contrast, the more heroic traditions lingered on in the cultures of the continent, where considerable contempt was expressed by its poets and philosophers for "mere" material interests—as when Johann von Schiller, quoted by Hirschman, exclaims in a lament:

> For the world is ruled only by interest.[42]

One cannot read the essays of Hume without discerning their moral force and that of his admirable life;[43] one cannot confine him in the narrow, pinched vision that Hirschman appears to assert. Nor can one read Smith's *Theory of Moral Sentiments* or parallel passages in *The Wealth of Nations* without discerning that Smith held material interests as but a *means* to the good life, of which the perfection of human sentiments in a full and disinterested sympathy was for him (and for British moralists generally) the highest form of life.

True enough, Hume, Smith, and other British moralists saw in a regime anchored in commerce, with the political objective of producting plenty, an improvement of human social life, beyond the calamitous circumstances that had preceded it in all known regimes. Hirschman himself retains, however, a sort of continental, aristocratic disdain for such a regime. Nor does he recognize that Hume and Smith use even such loaded words as "avarice" and "acquisitiveness" in two quite different senses. As Hume's essay on avarice demonstrates, such words were sometimes given a negative meaning akin to miserliness, graspingness, and self-centeredness, especially under regimes of scarcity and narrow horizons. But when Hume and Smith use these words with a positive connotation, they are thinking of utterly different circumstances and utterly different sentiments. The drive to better one's condition is not itself evil but good; even professors of intellectual history need not be ashamed to share in it.

It is, in fact, the characteristic of self-consciously revolutionary thinkers, as Hume and Smith knew themselves to be, that they can scarcely resist turning the highly charged meanings of the established order on their head, in order to transvalue them. What earlier moralists had considered "the most vulgar and the most obvious," Smith was explicitly willing to make the humble foundation of his system. He thus dared traditionalists to argue that it is wrong for ordinary people, most of them trapped in mean circumstances, "to propose and to wish the bettering of their condition." And if more material comfort is seen by "the great part of men" as a means of bettering their condition, it does not follow that it is the full and final end of what they propose and wish to achieve.

In fact, one of the untold stories of capitalist development—a story ideologically resisted by traditionalists and Socialists alike—would display the broadminded and humane concerns that it inspired in the growing middle class: not least, a concern for the deplorable state of the poor, *les misérables*, under earlier regimes. In advancing their argument, Hume and Smith had in truth the plight of the poor as a main concern. Regularly, they attacked the moral standing of traditionalist moralists by asking what *their* regimes had done for the slaves, the impoverished, and the vast masses of the poor on whom their own regimes rested and whom they had recruited as soldiers in pursuit of their destructive passions.

Yet it was not only the raising up of the poor that Hume and Smith envisaged in "arguing for capitalism before its triumph." They also had in mind the surge of spiritual independence and the extension of humane sympathies that would flow, they predicted, from the sway of a more free and beneficent regime. Smith saw his own life's works as moral teaching for the "new class" of his era: that of the jurists, entrepreneurs, industrialists, merchants, bankers, and civil servants, whose numerical growth he was championing in Scotland (and by the implication of his classic work, in all nations).[44] From this large-minded conception of the capitalist ethos flowed the multitudes of unprecedented and sympathy-expanding studies on which Friedrich Engels drew (for antagonistic purposes) in his *Condition of the Working Class in England*. There flowed steady advances in the care of eyes, teeth, and all the ailments to which common people are prey. And there flowed, as well, such fundamental institutions as the free press, an emphasis upon education (not least, in Smith, for the new industrial workers), and the general pattern of upward social and cultural striving. Hirschman writes as if to demean the bourgeois revolution by interpreting it in the most narrow way possible. He fails to see the humane grandeur of its purposes and its historical achievements.

The Bourgeois Revolution

Yet what Hirschman leaves out of his nonetheless useful analysis, the contemporary world has not failed to see. For it has turned out that the citizens of Estonia, Latvia, and Lithuania, of Poland and Hungary, and even of Russia and China themselves, *do* seem "to propose and to wish to better their condition"—and so, it seems, do virtually all the peoples of the world. Most vulgar and most obvious this basic wish may seem, and yet, amazingly, the artists, scholars, and intellectuals of the West seem unaccountably ashamed to be implicated in promoting the fulfillment of this wish. A recent cartoon by Jules Feiffer catches this treason of the clerks succinctly. A black-garbed, bearded artist, brush in hand cries out in successive panels:

My art exposes your commercialism/
your overindulgence—materialism/
acquisitiveness/
your greed, your narcissim/
Your corrupt ethics—morality/
I dedicate my life as an artist to the free expression of
my contempt for what you are/
Fund me.[45]

Confronted, then, by a planet on which most fellow humans live in conditions too appalling to countenance, what do these enemies of capitalism, even now after its triumph, propose to offer them: the stone of socialism? the scandal of traditional precapitalist economies ruled by the passions of *caudillos* and tribal chiefs?

Since the bold theorists of the seventeenth and eighteenth centuries humanely sketched them out, the full moral resources of the capitalist revolution have never yet been plumbed. This may be explainable by downward mobility in the status of all aristocracies, including that of artists and intellectuals, whose tradition it was to celebrate the aristocracy while making the bourgeoisie their sworn enemy. Abundant evidence for this assertion lies in the contempt almost universally shown by artists and intellectuals for the bourgeoisie and their commerce and their industry—and for their manifold and obvious virtues even more than for their often glaring (and self-admitted) faults. I doubt if any leading class in history except this new and humane middle class has more patiently borne, and more self-critically enjoyed, the mockery that artists have constantly heaped upon them; they have even paid for it.

And yet behind the bourgeois ethos lies a thick web of classic and traditional assumptions: that all human beings are of one interdependent family; that all experience upward strivings, both material and spiritual; that a precondition of self-governance and life under regimes formed "by the consent of the governed" is an economy of openness and "plenty"; that the rights of minorities—individual rights, even—are coequal with the public good as twin objects for the protection of governments; that human rights are, in practice, best protected under conditions of economic independence for the many, with checks and balances against political ambition; that the pursuit of plenty, while an indispensable means to humankind's flourishing, is not an end in itself, but only a beginning in the voyage to expand and to deepen human sympathies; and that "freedom" is not solely freedom from want and tyranny, but also that exercise of ancient virtues such as honesty, courage, justice, and sober temperance that alone enables men and women to use their full capacity for human liberty.

The bourgeois revolution is, then, no mean and petty thing. From often brutal experience, citizens around the world have come to discern quite clearly both the illusions of salvation through politics and the suffocating limits of mere economism. Thus, in its contemporary stage the bourgeois revolution has opened up before us the realm of moral and cultural development. Here is where true moral primacy lies, now as ever: in the groping sense among hundreds of millions of economically liberated persons that plenty is only a means and that the true vocation of free peoples lies in the achievement of those inner strengths that give acts of liberty their beauty—those practices of sobriety, justice, and generosity that our nature commands. Failing these, humans have missed the point of liberty.

For if by contrast with the pursuit of power, glory, and passion the systematic pursuit of wealth represented a fundamental improvement in the human understanding of the path toward virtue, in itself it is only the threshold. We must step through it to confront our most urgent and broadly perceived social worry today: the disorder and missed possibilities of our moral lives. Hume, Smith, and others correctly perceived wealth to be a useful means for opening up to all, and not merely to aristocrats, the pursuit of virtue. Now the vista they opened up—self-education in moral virtue—lies before us. The world's peoples seem to sense this and to express an almost universal disaffection with the merely economic and political "salvation myths" that devastated the modern world.

"The revolution," to repeat my favorite saying from the poet Charles Peguy, "is moral or not at all."

The Future Task for Religious Ethics

It follows from this brief survey of the eighteenth-century Scottish revolution in ethical thinking regarding the creation of wealth that the ethical teaching of Christians and Jews need not, with respect to economics, begin from scratch. In the precapitalist world of almost universal poverty, a world that gave little thought to the systematic creation of wealth, it may have been understandable to focus ethical reflection chiefly upon remedies for misery. For some, it remains a great temptation to continue in precapitalist modes of thinking even today. The dream of socialism, rooted in certain flawed economic doctrines of the nineteenth century, heightened that temptation. That dream has ended in the last part of the twentieth century in a nightmare—in China, in the Soviet Union, in Eastern Europe, and in all the scattered Marxist nations. "If you socialized the Sahara," a mordant Eastern European proverb has it, "in ten years there would be a shortage of sand."

We read, for example, of unbelievable shortages of soap, medicines, and other basic items of everyday living in Poland and the USSR. Shelves in stores are empty. Basic foods are scarce. Dental care proceeds without anesthetics. Such goods as are produced are of inferior, sometimes hardly usable quality. According to a detailed report by Zbigniew Bochniarz of the University of Minnesota's Hubert Humphrey Institute:

27 areas containing a third of Poland's population are regarded as "ecological hazards" due to multiple violations of standards. Norms are consistently exceeded at 60% of nitrogen oxide monitoring sites and 80% of those for dust and soot emissions. Four-fifths of Poland's soils have become highly acidified; 70% of its southern forests are projected to die by century's end. Between 1965 and 1985, Polish waters fit for human consumption dropped from 33% to 6% of all surface waters, while those unfit even for industry use nearly doubled.

Poland produces about 20 times more soot and five times more sulfur dioxide and solid waste per unit of gross national product than does Western Europe. Its mortality rate for males over 35 is about 50% higher than West Germany's, and 50% higher in hazard areas than the national average. Since 1978, average annual growth rates for most pollutants have outstripped the growth of GNP.[46]

Meanwhile, even in the democratic and capitalist countries, men and women of enterprise work without the moral and intellectual support of thinkers and moralists. A capitalist system has come into being, but its moral purposes are left inarticulate. Serious Jews and Christians, asking for moral guidance in their wealth-creating activities, encounter silence, if not rejection. Obscurely, men and women of enterprise know that they are doing something valuable, but their efforts go without recognition, moral support, and ethical guidance.

The nine moral arguments on behalf of the establishment of creative economies I listed above have already been dimly grasped even in the citadels of Socialist society, in Hungary and Poland, in the Soviet Union, and among scholars in China. They are, however, seldom articulated.

Moreover, these nine arguments have profound theological warrant in Jewish and Christian theology. God created humans in his image: that is, to become creators. In the Jewish and Christian vision, human beings are born free and responsible. They have inalienable rights to life, liberty, and, as Pope John Paul II has recently emphasized, enterprise.[47] Systems of political economy need to be restructured to be worthy of these images of God. Since vast poverty still exists on earth and since the needs of this earth's ever-larger population continue to grow, a full-fledged Jewish and Christian ethic of wealth production clearly needs to be developed, along with systems designed to encourage it and the practices and habits that both allow it to take place and make it more and more humane.

To be sure, the augmentation of fortune is but a means; but it is a necessary means. Like every other human virtue, it is subject to corruption and misuse, and those abuses must be guarded against. The best moral instruction, however, begins by raising aloft the ideal to be pursued: the exercise of God-given talents to imagine, invent, discover, and bring into widespread use the resources that God has hidden in the natural world. To help to develop in all humans the virtue of enterprise, that they might exercise their creative capacities, is a task far from yet being accomplished. Institutional supports for this virtue need to be imagined, experimented with, and made to work. These include accessible, quick, and inexpensive ways to incorporate new businesses; institutions of credit, especially for the poor; markets open to the poor; an education in the moral and intellectual virtues of enterprise; and the transmission of skills in every field of economic creativity. Further, no society ought to depend on a relatively small economic elite only; all citizens, especially the poor, should be brought into participation in enterprising, wealth-creating activities,[48] and all those other creative endeavors that make the environment of work humane. Every man and woman has a fundamental human right to personal economic enterprise. Existing systems should be scrutinized in the light of how they assist, or block, the free exercise of that right.

In short, humans were not created to be receivers only, or clients only, but also creators. God gave them minds and imaginations, as well as courage and a zest for trial and error. He implanted in them a desire to better their condition, for their families and for the whole of human society. The creation of wealth is a social task and the supportive efforts of all are necessary to its accomplishment. It is especially necessary for the poor. Since we now know that wealth can be created in a sustained and systematic way, then—given the immense suffering of so many poor—economic development has become a moral obligation. We are obliged to work to shape institutions and systems that permit its flourishing. The cost, otherwise, is widespread misery, from which so much of the world today, lacking such institutions, unnecessarily suffers.

Both the traditionalist economic vision and the Socialist economic vision have proved inadequate. The capacity of capitalist and democratic systems to raise up hundreds of millions of the poor has been abundantly proved. Such systems do not promise, or deliver, paradise on earth. They are but instruments of our larger moral and cultural purposes. But it is precisely the leaders and thinkers of the moral and cultural sectors of the free societies that have been most deficient in grasping the moral and spiritual possibilities these novel systems of political economy have opened up before us. The thinkers of the Scottish Enlightenment achieved an unprecedented revolution in the human ethos, whose spiritual possibilities have yet to be realized. It is my hope that moral and cultural leaders, philosophers and poets, theologians and prelates, will awaken from their slumbers, grasp these possibilities, and fashion from them maxims of practical moral guidance, for which so many economic activists are manifestly thirsty. In Latin America as in North America, we badly need this moral awakening.

8
The Moral, Cultural, and Political Responsibilities of Business

In the year 1800, only 900 million persons inhabited this entire planet. Nearly all lived in poverty, suffered precarious health, were illiterate, and under tyranny. The average age at death was about eighteen. To get between any two cities, methods of transport were still roughly as they had been in the time of Christ—by foot, or beast, or horse-drawn carriage. Eyeglasses were barely available. Almost universally, teeth were bad, dental care unknown.

Yet look around us today. Since 1800, enormous progress has been made—most spectacularly in economics and its attendant blessings in medicine, transport, and communications. Today, the planet supports not 900 million but 4.9 *billion* persons. And their average life expectancy has climbed to fifty-nine (in Latin America to sixty-five). Progress has occurred in many places on this planet in political liberties, the protection of rights, and the institutions of moral and cultural pluralism. There remains much to be done. But progress during a very brief span of history has been immense.

How did this progress happen? The one-word answer to that question is *system*. Progress occurred systematically; it occurred because of system.

The Importance of System

Beginning in the seventeenth and eighteenth centuries, human beings began to figure out, through trial and error, certain secrets of politics and economics. They began with what, under the teachings of Judaism and Christianity, had become to them a self-evident truth, articulated in this way:

> that all Men are created equal, that they are endowed by their Creator with certain unalienable Rights; . . . That to secure these rights, Governments are instituted among Men, deriving their just Powers from the Consent of the Governed.

At that time, believers in such truths faced a practical, systemic problem. Granted, each human being is made in the image of God.

Granted, each is made to be a creator, in the image of God. How, then, do these believers constitute systems of political economy worthy of such creatures? How can a system of political economy be matched to the capacities of free, responsible, creative citizens?

A second systemic question was also asked: What are the nature and the cause of the wealth of nations? How can a system be designed so that it liberates and nourishes the causes of wealth, among all the peoples on earth? How can immemorial poverty be eliminated? How can the poor of the world be liberated, so they are no longer poor?

The answer to what causes the wealth of nations is deceptively simple. That cause is intellect: that is, invention, innovation, the creativity of the human mind.

Through these two questions, humanity at last came to the essential architecture for social systems designed to liberate men and women everywhere—as we have seen, to liberate them from torture and tyranny through concrete political institutions; to liberate them from poverty through specific economic institutions; and to liberate their minds, imaginations, and freedom of expression through institutions of pluralism.

We human beings are three-sided beings. We are, simultaneously, political animals seeking liberty and justice for all; economic animals seeking sustained humane development and liberation from poverty; and inquiring, truth-seeking, symbol-making animals seeking to follow conscience and to come, as Jews and Christians believe, to the vision of God. In every corner of our three-sided nature, we human beings seek to be ourselves: that is, to be reflective and to choose—to create freely our own destiny.

For this reason, any social system that would truly liberate us to be ourselves must also be a three-sided system. It must secure our political rights, our economic rights, and our moral and cultural rights. It must nurture our capacities for liberty, responsibility, and growth in all three spheres: political, economic, and moral and cultural.

An intellectual tragedy occurred, however, shortly after these discoveries were made. These three essential social systems were parceled out to different branches of inquiry. Political scientists took over the study of politics; economists took over the study of economics; and philosophers, theologians, historians, artists, and literary persons took over the fields of morals and culture—and often in separation from one another. For purposes of a division of labor, these separations make sense. Each of these fields is enormous in itself; each takes years to master. But in real life no one of us can live three separate lives. Each human being is simultaneously a political citizen, an economic agent, and a carrier of morals and culture. We are not internally divided into three; we are one. In each life, all three sets of human responsibilities must be united. To live as free men and women, we must take up our responsibilities in all three fields.

One result of modern specialization, however, is that each of us sometimes develops one dimension of life far more highly than the other two. Some of us, for example, might become so preoccupied with economic issues and business problems that we neglect our responsibilities in the other two dimensions. The same temptation, of course, occurs within the other specializations. Often those in politics or those immersed in morals and culture are woefully under-developed in their understanding of economic reality.

These questions of personal conscience concern how each of us might wisely distribute our energies in fulfilling all three of our responsibilities, as political citizens, as economic agents, and as bearers of moral and cultural responsibilities. These questions are important, even indispensable. A question of greater generality, however, must be asked: What is the responsibility of the business system—of businesses, of private economic corporations—to the political system and to the moral and cultural system of which it is a part?

A Free Private Sector—Rare and Fragile

Over large stretches of this planet, private business corporations are barely allowed to function, or not allowed at all. In Socialist systems of the Marxist-Leninist type, economic activities are entirely con-trolled by the state and owned by the state, except for a very limited number of private enterprises. (In China, for example, a nation of 1 billion persons, only 24 million workers are employed in privately owned businesses.)[1] To be sure, Socialist leaders today recognize that the cause of economic progress is the creativity of the free mind. Both in the Soviet Union and even more in China, the basic facts of human nature are breaking through the fog of ideology.

Freedom works, invention works, innovation works, enterprise works. Both Deng Xiaoping (until Tiananmen Square) and Gorbachev by the late 1980s recognized these facts. How far they were willing to diminish state and party power to reap the fruits of the creativity of free private citizens was long in doubt. But they had begun, at least, to learn the lesson articulated so clearly by Pope John Paul II about *the right of economic initiative.*[2]

Yet the Socialist states based upon Marxism-Leninism are not the only states in the world that suppress the right to personal economic enterprise and initiative that makes human beings images of the

91

Creator. Many traditionalist societies do the same. One sees this in many parts of Asia, Africa, and Latin America.

This Western Hemisphere of ours is the "hemisphere of liberty," but not yet the hemisphere of economic liberty. Many of the nations in our hemisphere are still heavily statist in the traditional, premodern way. In Peru, for example, millions of economic agents, prevented from incorporating their own businesses legally, are forced to work as "illegals." Half the housing in Lima is built by illegals; 95 percent of the public transport is run by illegals.[3] How sad it is that so many economically productive citizens are obliged to work outside the law, because the traditional laws of mercantilist governments keep them outside the law.

I have heard some Latin American priests say that Latin America's problem is "savage capitalism." In fact, the reality may be savage but it is not capitalist. Most of the nations of Latin America are mercantilist, almost patrimonial in structure; the economic activities of their citizens are heavily abridged, limited, and controlled by state officials. The precapitalist, mercantilist model that was common in the centuries before economic liberation is still potent.[4] In most of Latin America, capitalism—the system based upon the right to personal economic initiative and the creativity of the human mind—has not yet arrived.

To have a market system, to respect private property, and to permit private profits—all these do not capitalism make. On the contrary, these minimal characteristics are common to all traditionalist, precapitalist, state-controlled economies. Capitalism begins when the right to personal economic initiative is protected and nourished; when economic activities, while subject to fruitful regulation, are liberated from state oppression; and when the cause of wealth—the creativity of the imagination and mind of every citizen—is given its rightful liberty.[5]

The term *rightful liberty* denotes, as our patriotic hymn in the United States puts it, "liberty in law." The liberty that nourishes creativity, invention, and innovation and that allows the moral virtue of enterprise to flourish is *not* libertinism, or hedonism, or egotism, but liberty under law, raising the level of the common good.

As we have seen, enterprise is a new moral virtue, not found in the classical list of the virtues. It means the moral and intellectual habit of being alert, noticing, discerning new possibilities. It is the habit appropriate to creativity in the arts, to the discernment of creative and productive paths amid the perplexities of politics, and to invention and innovation in economics. Enterprise is a moral virtue that could scarcely be celebrated in the traditional society, since such societies were for centuries relatively stable and unchanging and their citizens were expected to follow custom, to keep the rules, and to obey authorities. Few in those days were taught the virtue of enterprise. (A wit has said the classic role of the ordinary citizen was: "Pray, pay, and obey.")

Enterprise is, rather, the intellectual and moral virtue appropriate to free societies, prompting citizens everywhere to invent, to innovate, and to exercise creativity. A citizen in the traditional society did not need enterprise, because there was no scope for it. In a free, dynamic society, the virtue of enterprise is necessary for every able-bodied person, if all are to participate in the common project of advancing social development.

Enterprise is a fundamental human right. It is also an intellectual and moral virtue that can be taught. Like every other virtue, it needs institutions to secure it, to nourish it, and to bring it to full flower. For virtues are never merely private. They require social support: social structure, legitimation, and institutional expression. A society that depends upon universal participation in economic life must teach this intellectual and moral virtue, protect its public exercise by law, prevent its oppression, and open access to it.

In the real world, the exercise of enterprise has necessary preconditions. Before they can exercise their God-given capacities for enterprise, the poor usually need access to credit at affordable interest rates. In this one critical respect, capital comes before labor. Before a product is produced, the materials for it must typically be purchased on credit, which is later repaid from the profit on their sale. Thus before the poor can sell the products they create, they need the means to create them, and to obtain these means they need access to credit. The virtue of enterprise is not only personal but social and cannot be exercised except within a social system that makes credit universally available, especially to the poor.

It is important, then, to underline the importance of system. What makes dynamic economic development occur is enterprise, but enterprise, in turn, depends upon nourishment from its surrounding political and moral-cultural system. In the Soviet Union, General Secretary Gorbachev publicly complains that there is almost no sign of enterprise. The economy stagnates and is, he says, in dangerous decline. As the joke among Soviet workers goes: "We pretend to work, and they pretend to pay us." How can anyone exercise enterprise when he or she is not allowed to make personal decisions and daily meets only disincentives? The exercise of enterprise depends upon a nurturing political and moral system.

It follows that in a commercial republic whose economic dynamism depends upon personal enterprise, we each must be concerned about the health of the political system and of the moral system in which the economic system lives and moves. Where the political system is hostile to enterprise and where the moral and cultural system condemns enterprise, enterprise cannot flower. Whoever favors the right of personal enterprise must take responsibility for surrounding it with a political system and a moral-cultural system that allow it to flourish.

This is the fundamental reason that economists must not be concerned solely with economics and that men and women of business must not be concerned solely with business. Every economic system depends on the political system and the moral system within which it is embodied. Therefore, persons in business must take responsibility for politics and for the moral-cultural system. Not to do so would be suicidal.

Furthermore, the chief historical justification for an economy based upon the fundamental human right to personal economic initiative is that it serves the common good. Above all, it raises up the poor. Until the end of the eighteenth century, it was thought that nothing could be done to change the suffering of the poor. The philosopher Hannah Arendt has written that a decisive point in world history occurred when America showed that people, once poor, could move out of poverty en masse. This new fact broke the ancient spell that held grinding poverty to be natural, inevitable, and unchangeable. After the American experience, poverty was no longer excusable, and thus "the social question" was raised for the whole world.[6]

For anyone concerned about a healthy business system, then, it is suicidal to overlook the rapid economic development of the poor. The right to personal economic initiative belongs especially to the poor, begins among the poor, and allows the poor to participate in economic dynamism. Nothing less than legal and institutional support for that right will permit the poor to exercise this God-given right. A truly free and dynamic society needs the participation of the poor. The greater the reach of economic activism among the poor, the larger the national market. Businessmen, above all, far more than politicians or professors, depend upon growing prosperity among the poor.

This last point bears elaboration. An Italian Communist once explained to me during a television debate in Italy: "You capitalists fail to make one strong point in your favor. In Italy, the effect of capitalism has been to make the workers middle class, depriving us of a proletariat. Now the people our party organizes best are students, clergymen, and professors." This is a variation on the point made by the Yugoslav philosopher Milovan Djilas in *The New Class*.[7] When modern societies educate larger numbers of citizens and when modern governments employ a high proportion of all workers, they create a "new class," composed of workers in the "knowledge industry," "communications industry," and government. This new class generally has a strong material and ideological interest in big government and in the state-centered management of other citizens. Its interests lie less with the classic working class, less with small business, less with large corporations and more with the state bureaucracy, state-owned corporations, and state banks. This new class is powerful. It forms a new elite whose leading members are not only highly educated and skilled in articulating ideas and policy but very powerful in directing public opinion. In other words, this new class has become in many ways the most powerful class in modern societies.

Moreover, this new class often speaks about the poor, using them as a rhetorical instrument of its own power. Typically, though, its recommendations offer little that will actually help the poor to cease being poor or help the poor become more active and effective in achieving economic liberation. In practice, the new class often favors a "managed" poor, rather than a self-sufficient independent poor.

This new class is primarily moved by, and preoccupied with, ideas. Although historically attracted to statism, many of its members have in recent years come to see statism as a mistake. They reject the idea that "progress" means greater power for the state. Instead, for them, the new idea of progress is rooted in the creativity of every single human person—in economic enterprise, in political democracy, and in a more active, energetic, and civil pluralism of open discussion. Thus, even in the USSR, "liberal" has become a good word, and "liberalization," "openness," "privatization," "initiative," and "enterprise" signify powerful new forces of progress, rooted in the individual mind and imagination.

Since the new class is open to fresh ideas, it may very well choose liberty over statism, "seek truth through facts" (Deng Xiaoping), and learn from reality itself that the liberation of the poor is best achieved through empowering the poor to use their vast economic creativity. Most of the poor, in fact, are not proletarians, but micro-entrepreneurs. They need a system favorable to small enterprises. More and more intellectuals around the world are coming to see this, often through the failure of other methods.

The rise of the new class creates a new situation for leaders of business enterprises. For the chief weapon of the new class is ideas,

ideas that may either strengthen the power of the traditional state or, on the contrary, open up new scope for economic liberty.

Most persons in business are poorly prepared to do battle in the world of ideas. Preeminently practical persons, they are often inarticulate in an unfamiliar context. Sometimes they are not well read and do not even know the basic arguments. They defend themselves badly, not even recognizing how important their own work is in liberating the poor from the bondage of traditional poverty.

In Latin America, for instance, millions upon millions of able-bodied adults are either unemployed or underemployed. Who will create new jobs for these millions? Who will help to stimulate and to support the millions of new enterprises necessary to achieve full employment? Meanwhile, there is also an immense amount of work to be done. Millions of homes need to be built and better furnished. Roads and streets need to be paved. Millions of citizens lack basic household goods—electricity, a refrigerator, a good stove, and the like. Who will bring these two resources together—creative work to be done and unemployed workers—if not men and women of enterprise, of imagination, and of know-how? The liberation of the poor in Latin America depends, more than on any other factor, upon the creativity of business men and women in the private sector. Their responsibilities for the fate of the poor in Latin America are immense. Their vocation is a noble one, because the poor depend much more upon them than upon government, or upon the new class, or upon anyone else. But business people must come to the aid of the poor both in the world of fact and in the world of ideas. They must join these two together: the work to be done with the workers to do it.

For this reason, especially, one of the major responsibilities of business leaders today lies in the world of ideas, a new terrain for them. They must be the architects of liberation, offering a vision of how the poor will be liberated from traditional poverty to become economically creative. Business leaders must invent institutions of credit, of cheap and easy legal incorporation, of training in skills and in methods, so that the poor can begin to exercise their fundamental, God-given right to personal economic initiative. If business leaders do not do this, who will? Government cannot do it. The new class shows few signs, so far, of even thinking about it. The chief responsibility falls upon the leaders of the private sector.

Moreover, to help the poor is to help businessmen. In this respect, free economies have one happy characteristic that many analysts have failed to note: the success of every person is enhanced, not diminished, by the success of all others. This has meant a revolution in ideas—in fact, not one revolution but three.

The Three Revolutions in Thinking

Under precapitalist systems, the secrets of creating new wealth were not known and the existing sum of wealth was relatively fixed. For some to become wealthy, others had to become poor. The principal way to acquire wealth was to *take* it from others. When new wealth could not be created—through invention or innovation—how else could it be acquired, except by taking?

Today that situation has been reversed. A society based upon creating new wealth by invention, innovation, and enterprise has a totally different moral basis. New wealth can be created without diminishing preexisting wealth. Every increment of new wealth by one person opens up new opportunities and possibilities for others. The success of each furthers the success of all. The higher the standard of living and the greater the economic activism of the poor, the more dynamic and wealthy every other part of society becomes. People too poor to supply a market for goods and services lower the horizon for business prospects. As the poor rise to middle-class status, markets expand. The most prosperous economic environment is one in which all participate and all benefit.

This revolution in world thinking is too little noted—this move from wealth as piracy to wealth as new creation benefiting all. But it was not unconscious. As long ago as 1742 David Hume grasped the new way of thinking:

> I shall therefore venture to acknowledge, that, not only as a man, but as a British subject, I pray for the flourishing commerce of Germany, Spain, Italy, and even France itself. I am at least certain that all nations would flourish more with such enlarged and benevolent sympathies toward each other.[8]

And as recently as the 1930s, the often leftward-leaning American journalist Walter Lippmann saw this revolution at work. Given reliance upon creating new wealth, he noted, rather than reliance upon redividing what already exists,

> For the first time in human history men had come upon a way of producing wealth in which the good fortune of others multiplied their own. . . . They actually felt it to be true that an enlightened self-interest promoted the common good. For the first time men could conceive a social order in which the ancient moral aspiration for liberty, equality, and fraternity was consistent with the abolition of poverty and the increase of wealth.[9]

More recent is the revolution in ideas about politics. Although it seemed obvious to the first liberals that economic freedom goes hand in hand with political freedom, ideologues in recent decades have sometimes said that a free capitalist economy depends upon political dictatorship. History has decided that question otherwise. Empirically, it is now clear that a free capitalist economy is a necessary but not sufficient condition for political democracy and that democracy is necessary for the long-term durability of capitalism. The two go together: capitalism, democracy. For this reason, I prefer to speak of "democratic capitalism" rather than of free enterprise alone.

As economic development proceeds worldwide, pressures for democratization rise. This has happened in Greece, Spain, Portugal, the Philippines, South Korea, Chile, and many other places. The reason is plain. Successful leaders of a middle class that grows larger and stronger begin to believe that they are smarter than any dictator. They want to govern themselves. They begin to insist upon self-government as the only form of polity truly consistent with their economic and moral and cultural liberties—consistent, indeed, with their self-respect.

Furthermore, in those cases in which dictators have been long in power—Singapore is one case, South Korea until recently was another—the problems of a peaceful and orderly transition from one leader to another became so severe that they threatened to undermine economic progress and civil harmony. Thus, a second empirical proposition has been observed, which complements the first: constitutional democracy is a necessary but not sufficient condition for stable economic development. Democracy is especially necessary for making transitions in leadership constitutional, regular, frequent, and routine. Otherwise, the threat of instability cripples free and secure long-range thinking.

In summary, a free capitalist economy requires democracy, and democracy requires a free capitalist economy. As the distinguished sociologist Peter Berger points out in his study *The Capitalist Revolution*, these propositions are not ideological; they now have empirical warrant and would be overturned by facts to the contrary.[10]

Finally, we turn to the revolution of ideas in morals and culture. In our time, intelligent Socialists have also come to reject the utopianism and wishful thinking of primitive socialism. Consider the actions of François Mitterrand in France, Felipe Gonzalez in Spain, Mario Soares in Portugal, and the public statements of Gorbachev and the former Socialists of Hungary, Poland, and Czechoslovakia. More and more, Socialist leaders not only turn to markets, private property, incentives, and profit systems, as the only proven and effective means of ending economic stagnation and generating economic growth, but also speak clearly about the role of freedom of thought and expression, inquiry and imagination, enterprise and initiative, in the creation of new wealth. Morally and culturally, economic facts have spoken for themselves. More and more, Socialist leaders talking about economics sound like Ronald Reagan. Over time, reality speaks louder than ideology.

Thus, we live in a very fertile period. Realists of all persuasions may be able to come together on fairly common ground—with important disagreements but with certain shared goals. I emphasize four well-established points of agreement:

• For the poor to cease being poor, economic creativity is indispensable.

• For a creative, dynamic, broadly based economic system, the surrounding political system and moral-cultural system must nourish the fundamental human right of every citizen to economic initiative and enterprise.

• The more active the poor become as creators of new wealth, the larger markets also become. Under the new economic realism, the success of all enhances the success of each.

• Business leaders are committing collective suicide if they attend only to business. They must create conditions of liberty both in the political system and in the moral-cultural system. To do this, they must become more involved than ever before in the world of ideas, especially of ideas about system. They must work for a system of ordered and creative liberty in every sphere.

This "hemisphere of liberty" requires systems of liberty, worthy of all its citizens, each of whom was made in the image of the Creator: the Creator of two large and incredibly beautiful continents, strung together as if they had always been intended to be holding hands in liberty.

9
The Economic Preconditions
of Democracy

In this concluding chapter, I would like to summarize some of the themes of the preceding chapters and offer a concrete political program for the future. The changes that I have in mind are revolutionary in scope, but peaceable in practice. They would fundamentally alter the precapitalist systems of Latin America and transform them into dynamic foundations for political liberty.

When we inquire into the economic preconditions of democracy, it is most illuminating to do so from the point of view of the poor. Nothing makes democracy more beloved to the poor than the ability of families at the bottom of society to better their economic condition from decade to decade. Nothing so sours the poor on democracy as the experience of economic stagnation or decline. More even than others in society, the poor have a need to experience tangible economic progress in their own lives. They do not expect paradise on earth, but they do expect a horizon of continuing improvement. Therefore, democracy without economic progress for the poor is not likely to be sustainable, since it cannot win the love necessary to its own continuance.

Democracy and Capitalism

This is the reason, perhaps, why all the stable and long-lived democracies in the world have occurred on the firm and dynamic base of capitalist economies. It is also the reason, surely, why democracies in Latin America have heretofore proved so fragile. Nothing is more certain in Latin America today, as Octavio Paz has wisely written, than that the idea of democracy has captured the hearts and minds of large majorities of the people.[1] In this hemisphere, and now perhaps worldwide, no other form of government has achieved the same profound sense of legitimacy. Yet one secret crucial to the sustenance of Latin American democracies has so far been elusive. It is the economic part of the twin concept, political economy. The people of Latin America take quickly to democracy. They have not yet learned to make their economies show steady, visible progress for the poor at the bottom of society.

On these counts, too, though, progress has been made. It is wrong to underestimate the real improvement in Latin America since World War II in economic growth, in the expansion of education, in better health, and in greater average longevity. Much more credit is due for this progress than, in prolonged bouts of self-criticism, is usually given. Nonetheless, the numbers of the very poor, the destitute, the unemployed, and the underemployed remain uncommonly large. If we are to think about the economic future of Latin American democracies, we need to think first of all about the economic future of the poor.

Many of us are much indebted to Hernando de Soto's *The Other Path*, and to Mario Vargas Llosa's gracious introduction to its English edition, for its depiction of the circumstances of the poor of Peru.[2] Others in Latin America have commented that this depiction is also valid, *mutatis mutandis*, for the poor of their own nations. What leaps out from such discussions is the amazing extent to which the poor of Latin America are deprived of economic liberty. Even under conditions of democracy and political liberty, many are not free economically: not free to incorporate their own small businesses; to toil legally, with full standing in the law, in their own active enterprises; to have access, legally and cheaply, to the credit that is necessary for dynamic economic activities, since they begin as creative ideas long before goods or services can be produced for sale and profit; and to exercise, in short, what Pope John Paul II has called the fundamental "right of economic initiative." Lacking such economic liberties, how can their political liberties long survive? How can their political liberties win from them their full-hearted love?

Surely, the lessons of the twentieth century have taught us that human liberty is of a piece. Liberty is, in fact, trinitarian. It has three coequal parts: political liberty, economic liberty, and moral and cultural liberty. Political liberty requires economic liberty. Both of these liberties require moral and cultural liberty—the liberty of responsibility, the liberty of the free mind and the free heart to reflect and to choose the paths of its own destiny. "The God who made us made us free"—morally free, politically free, economically free. One such freedom without the others is insufficient. It is insufficient not only in itself but also as a protection of the other two. Each of the three liberties needs the other two for its own survival.

Perhaps because of the dreadful dangers of totalitarian modes of thinking in the twentieth century, we may have paid too much attention since World War II to political liberty and not enough to its preconditions, both moral and economic. The time is now past for that neglect. "Democracy" alone is now an insufficient battle cry. For democracy can scarcely be sustained where moral and economic liberties are not present. We may learn this to our sorrow in the present hopeful struggles for democracy in Eastern Europe and in Latin America.

Among the three liberties already mentioned, one alone (as we have seen) has primacy of place: moral, religious, cultural liberty—that is, the liberty to exercise human powers of reflection and of choice. In these two capacities, reflection and choice, each of us is made in the image of our Creator, whose two most favored names in the Jewish and Christian covenants are Light and Love. How to build a civilization more respectful of reflection and choice than any other in the annals of human history is our constant task.

By the freedom of the moral-cultural system, I mean the free exercise of conscience and the free flow of information and ideas. But I also mean freedom for the basic *institutions* of the moral-cultural sector—churches, families, universities, the press, and the other associations of spiritual, artistic, and cultural life. A totalitarian society tries to shut down this moral-cultural system. It suffocates it by depriving it of space. A free society allows it to grow, continually expanding civic space for the daily exercise of reflection and choice.

Human Capital

This primacy of the moral-cultural system carries over into economics. The primary cause of the wealth of nations (as we have seen) is human wit—discovery, invention, organization, enterprise. The number one resource of the free economy is *human capital*. Each nation's greatest single source of wealth is the creativity inalienably endowed in the heart and soul of every single person by the Creator. Its citizens are a nation's greatest economic resource. Each has been given by God the capacity to create more in a lifetime than he or she consumes. This is the very principle of human economic progress. Without it, economic development could not occur.

In almost every intellectual culture of the West, nonetheless, the true nature of the free economy is misperceived. Karl Marx tried to defile the name "capitalism" by defining it as an immoral force, by contrast with his own hazy utopia. Unfortunately, this Marxian utopia became—in the words of Vaclav Havel—a nightmare.[3] Worse still, Marxian definitions of reality have darkened even our own insight, blinding us to the true genius of the great economic discoveries of the West.

The Western vision of a free society—a free polity, a free economy, and a free and pluralistic moral-cultural system—is a vision of social justice. It is our dream that all nations shall grow in wealth and that the chains of material poverty should be lifted from every single family on earth. Nonetheless, a great many of our intellectuals, while willing to praise our moral-cultural and political ideals, have accepted a Marxist definition of our economic aims.

Most of our English-language dictionaries, for example, report a Marxist definition of capitalism. They define capitalism as a system of exchange through free markets, based upon private property, for purposes of profit or accumulation. This definition is an outrage. It does not even adequately distinguish capitalism from socialism (a system of exchange through command, based upon public owner-ship, for purposes of distribution). But it utterly fails to distinguish the newness and originality of capitalism from the premodern econ-omies of the ancient and medieval world. Markets, private property, and profits do not make a modern economy. And they certainly do not add up to capitalism. Virtually all precapitalist economies have these necessary, but not sufficient, characteristics. What is distinctive about the capitalist economy is its original discovery that the primary cause of economic development is mind. The cause of wealth is invention, discovery, enterprise.

This, incidentally, is why a capitalist system is so much fun. It brings delight to the inventive mind. It excites the creative capacities of ordinary people. It makes farmers more alert to small differences in seeds and soils and nutrients.[4] It makes citizens more aware of their own hidden capacities and of resources in their environment that are being overlooked. It makes men and women begin to study the needs and wants of others, to see whether there are goods or products not now available to them that would enhance their lives. A capitalist system is distinguishable among all others by the tide of invention and enterprise that sweeps through entire populations, transforming them from passivity to economic activism. A capitalist system begins from the bottom up; it raises up many rare talents for enterprise and invention among those born very poor. It normally begins, as Guy Sorman has felicitously put it, as "barefoot capital-ism."[5] Every citizen on earth has been endowed by God with the virtue of enterprise. An economic system that frees these citizens to exercise that inalienable capacity brings them delight.

It is not so easy, however, to design social systems that actually do liberate human beings for the free exercise of enterprise. Many nations on this planet have never yet done so. (In many languages, a good word for enterprise—the moral virtue of acting with personal initiative and creativity—is not easy to find because social conditions have repressed the reality to which such a word would point.) To erect social systems that promote and foster this important moral virtue is the single most important task for the party of liberty over the next ten years. The fate of democracy depends upon it.

A Practical Agenda

With this task in mind, I have tried to imagine a practical agenda for Eastern Europe, Latin America, and elsewhere, which consists of ten practical proposals. Like any moral virtue, enterprise develops far more broadly in a population where the social system does not punish it but undergirds and rewards it. To meet these two requirements, a society that wishes to build the economic foundations for a free polity will need to concentrate much effort on changing its social institutions and its laws.

Here, then, are ten practical proposals, a political platform for the party of liberty:

• to recognize in law the inalienable right of personal economic initiative

• to allow the multitudes who labor in the informal or illegal sector swift, easy, and inexpensive access to legal incorporation (ideally by mail, within fourteen days, for a modest registration fee of about U.S. $30)

• to empower all citizens now in the informal sector with all relevant legal and social supports for their economic activities and to build institutions designed to instruct them in how to make use of them

• to establish institutions of credit accessible to the poor, which also give professional advice on how to make their enterprises successful

• to favor by law and tax incentives virtually universal home ownership, land ownership, or both with full rights of ownership in perpetuity (including rights to buy or sell)

• to grant workers in state industries, utilities, and the like stock ownership in these enterprises, through employee stock ownership plans

• to sell off most state enterprises to the public, that is, to "privatize" them, through as wide a system of public ownership as possible, approximating universal participation in ownership

• to give primacy among social welfare expenditures to building systems of universal education, stressing the virtues of initiative, enterprise, invention, and social cooperation

• to strengthen the voluntary, nonstatist social sector by laws and tax incentives favorable to the development of foundations and other private institutes of social welfare, not as a substitute for state-sponsored social welfare programs, but as a fresh source of innovation and public service

• in recognition of their indispensable social contribution to the progress of science and the practical arts, to develop strong copyright and patent laws, which grant to authors and inventors the right to the fruits of their inventions for a limited time

This last element is one of the key turning points of economic revolution. It is decisive for the emergence of capitalism.

Conclusion

Liberty is many splendored. Political liberty depends on economic liberty. A capitalist, invention-centered economy is a necessary but not sufficient condition for democracy. Ordinary citizens judge a political economy by how well it enables them to exercise their own talents, including their capacity for economic enterprise. They depend upon the fruits of that enterprise, if they are to see their families better their condition from decade to decade. The poor, above all, want to see economic progress in the lives of their own families. To achieve this progress, a nation needs every one of its able-bodied citizens to exercise the creative imagination and economic energy that God has endowed in them. To be a vital political democracy, a nation also needs to be vital in its daily economic life—in every urban neighborhood, in every village, at every level of society.

Our German colleagues refer to the creative economy as "the social market economy." Others prefer to speak of the "free economy." For myself, to stress the creative, inventive, and enterprising character of the new economy, and to have a useful alternative to "democratic socialism" and "social democracy," I prefer to speak of "democratic capitalism." Still, the name we use is not so important as the underlying reality. That reality, in season and out, is the universal need for an inventive, enterprising economic system that will help the poorest in our midst to break the chains of poverty. Only a system that enables the poor to better their condition, and to see their children prosper, will win their love and enable them to exercise their political and moral liberties. Economic liberties may be the humblest liberties, but they are also basic. In the order of execution, they are probably the first that must be set in place, if the others are to flower. We cannot neglect them.

The revolution of liberty in this hemisphere is not yet complete. Each generation will have further work to do. Our hope must be that our own generation does its share and, if possible, a little more than its share.

Appendix

Thomas Aquinas, the First Whig

How do we do full justice to the spectacular revolution Thomas Aquinas wrought in his lifetime? We would be foolish to miss what he actually accomplished. Great minds like his remain alive as intimate partners in the centuries-long conversation in which our own minds are engaged.

We encounter the ideas of St. Thomas Aquinas in practically every court of law, in which criteria of full or diminished guilt are applied; in many attempts to contrive international law; in the conceptual separation of the things of God from matters proper to the state; in the use of concepts which he was the first to fashion and to order, such as "secular," "conscience," "will," and "person." Neither Dante in dramatic poetry nor St. John of the Cross in mysticism are conceivable apart from the labors of Aquinas. The Western tradition rests upon Aquinas as the sturdy bridge from the ancients (Moses and the prophets, the Greeks, Jesus, Cicero, and the great church fathers) to the modern age; he really did write a *Summa*, an architectural synthesis. Remove Aquinas and that bridge falls. Unlike Descartes, Hobbes, and other moderns, he really knew his ancients. A greater sophistication on their part might have saved generations of elementary confusions about the senses, the passions, the virtues, reason, and the like.

In this appendix, I would like to concentrate on only one achievement of Aquinas. My clue comes from Friedrich von Hayek, who, in the process of claiming for himself the noble name of "Whig" (in *The Constitution of Liberty*), cites as part of his own lineage Lord Acton's claim that St. Thomas Aquinas was "the first Whig."[1] What does this claim mean? In what sense is Aquinas entitled to it? To answer these questions, I think it best to capture first what Aquinas accomplished between his birth in 1224, just outside of Naples, and his death some forty-nine years later in 1274. I will conclude by situating the power of his thought in the Americas for the 1990s. The span of years between the lifetime of Aquinas and today, some 700 years, is about half the span between his lifetime and that of Aristotle, some 1,500 years.

The Battles Facing Aquinas

In 1245, at the age of twenty-one, Aquinas began his studies at the University of Paris. (In the prescribed Dominican manner, he walked to Paris from Naples.) The long missing text of Aristotle's *Nicomachean Ethics* had just been discovered after centuries of disappearance. The intellectual climate had otherwise been thoroughly permeated with studies of the Jewish and Christian books of the Bible and the church fathers, especially the Christian Platonists. Plato (at that time known only through the *Timaeus*) was referred to, for his mystical inclinations, as "the divine Plato," whereas Aristotle, known only for his books on logic, was called "the materialist" and the "atheist." Some of the authors that Aquinas studied upheld the thesis that, outside the grace of Christ, true virtue is not possible to human beings—indeed, that unless one professed Christian belief and was redeemed by grace, such sinfulness abounded that no one who was not a Christian could even be a true and full citizen.

Such pessimism, partly of an Augustinian coloring, made rough empirical sense. The evil that abounded in human beings in that semibarbarous age was everywhere apparent. The medieval schoolmen had a realistic view of the murders, rivalries, and debaucheries to which the most privileged of the day were especially prone. The man that Shakespeare was to call "the murdrous Machiavel" would soon describe multiple evils even in the papal court. Adultery and rape flourished. The walls of tiny mountain towns were necessarily thick and high, against the wantonness and violence rampant in the countryside. Such Christian peace as existed sought refuge in the cities; the very word "pagan" meant countryfolk, who were in many places thinly Christianized even into modern times (if such novels as *Christ Stopped at Eboli* are to be believed). To describe men as they actually behaved in the thirteenth century was not to hold an excessively optimistic view of human virtue. The rings of Dante's *Inferno*, the history of King Richard III, the depictions of hell on the frescoes of the Orvieto cathedral, and Michelangelo's Sistine Chapel do not describe paradise on earth.

By contrast, the vision of Aquinas was anything but bleak. Indeed, the sobriquet bestowed on him for his serenity was "the Angelic Doctor." This did not signify that he was otherworldly; indeed, he was rushed from one hot contemporary controversy and power struggle to another, dying, in fact, on his way to an embattled Council of the Church at Lyons. This epithet was intended, rather, to signify his uncommon capacities for the dispassionate assessment of evidence. He was famous for being able to do justice to more different points of view than any scholar before him (and maybe since).

In the matter that concerns us now—the just claims of nature within a world of grace—Aquinas was one of the first men in the Christian West to have in his hands an accurate Latin translation of Aristotle's *Ethics* and *Politics*. This translation was provided, at his request, by his schoolmate in Cologne, William Moerbeke, who like Aquinas had studied under the greatest and broadest mind of that generation, St. Albert the Great. Fortified by his own studies of Scripture, the church fathers, and in particular St. Augustine's eloquent writings on human weakness of will, Aquinas began his great commentaries on Aristotle's *Ethics*. Aristotle had been introduced to the West through Arab and Moslem commentaries, which suggested a kind of pantheism and materialism. Although the Arabic Aristotle was deeply troubling to the contemporary intellectual establishment, Aquinas found in the authentic text much that was invigorating. Whatever the biblical fundamentalists of his time might say, Aquinas had in hand manuscript proof of what Aristotle, while altogether unknowing of Moses, the prophets, and the teachings of Christ, could discern about the way human beings can and do act in the world. Aquinas found it morally admirable.

Quite independently of any biblical revelation, Aristotle had discerned what the Creator had written into the nature of his human creatures. Aquinas deeply honored this evidence. It helped him mightily in his own ability to understand Christian theology, to map out its relation to the works of (unaided) human intelligence. It raised many deeper questions about the Christian faith itself. It was, he thought, a priceless gift. Although his own life was built upon total commitment to the faith of Christ, he came to call Aristotle, in matters of unaided human wisdom—especially in matters that today we refer to as "the humanities"—*Magister*, the Teacher.

Aquinas, of course, never hesitated to go beyond Aristotle. Aquinas had, thanks to Jewish and Christian experience, much fuller and clearer notions than Aristotle of such basic ethical concepts as conscience, weakness of will, person, and community, among others. Above all, he had a less aristocratic, more egalitarian, sense concerning virtue and character. Aristotle had written for a special elite among men, the aristocratic warrior class, whereas Aquinas knew that Judaism and Christianity addressed widows, orphans, the poor, and indeed all human beings in their ordinariness.

Unhappily, Aquinas has come down to most American students as a philosopher rather than a theologian. Most read only what is of interest to the philosophy professors whose classes they take, usually such philosophical texts of Aquinas ripped from their theological context, horizon, and presuppositions as the treatise on law, the proofs for the existence of God, or the structure of human action. This is a certain denuding of Aquinas.

In addition, some of the greatest Thomists of our century happened to be philosophers: Etienne Gilson, Jacques Maritain, Anton Pegis, Yves R. Simon, Josef Pieper, and many others. All this is good and valuable. Still, when Aquinas is separated from the whole sweep of his theology—and, above all, from his mooring in *caritas* (that is, the love of God in which humans share)—a much thinner Aquinas emerges than the great intellectual figure that he actually is. And he is open to charges from theologians, who dismiss him as "just another Aristotle." In truth, Aquinas had to be deeper than Aristotle, more learned in traditions unknown to Aristotle, even to situate and to "rescue" Aristotle for the West. He had to make infinitely more distinctions and to account for many more materials than Aristotle had dealt with. To stand upon Aristotle's shoulders, he had to climb higher.

Although in what follows I intend to treat mainly worldly philosophical issues, to deal with Aquinas as "the first Whig," I omit much that could also be said *theologically* about some of these same issues. For it is rather from the philosophical terrain of his thought—specifically from his *political* philosophy—that the materials I extract are taken. Indeed, the very legitimacy of doing this is one of the great achievements Aquinas wrote into Christian intellectual history.

In addressing the thesis of his predecessors, that only those saved by the grace of Christ could be truly good men or good citizens of the earthly city, Aquinas pointed to manuscript evidence: the text of Aristotle showed how humans might follow the imperatives written into their nature to become good men and good citizens. Seeing that, Aquinas "saw that it was good." That alone might or might not be good enough for their salvation, depending on the invisible ways of grace spread by the Creator throughout the universe he had created and redeemed. If it was good enough for the Creator, that was plenty good for him—not sufficient, perhaps, for all purposes, but legitimately and fully good, and to be praised, as far as it went.

In other words, Aquinas distinguished "good" from "saved." He wished to honor the work of the Creator, and by no means at the expense of the Redeemer. It is the advantage of Jews and Christians, Aquinas argued, that "their God is reasonable."[2] (Albert Einstein was to pick up this line of thought in saying, "God does not play with dice.") Nature is good. Philosophy—proceeding by its own rules of evidence and proper methods—is good, not only good, but the highest and most legitimate of all human works, short of the works of faith. The vocation of philosopher—and scientist and artist—is a noble vocation for Christians to practice, good in itself, to be valued for itself, even as, properly coordinated, it can also be an instrument of, and is ordered to, the further riches of faith.

Faith, in short, does not contradict nature, nor the Redeemer the Creator. Faith does not contradict human knowledge or science; if it seems to, we must be missing something and need to think again on both sides. In God's eyes, the existing world is one, grasped in the eternal simultaneity of God's vision. To worship the true God, humans need not go down on all fours. The human that God loves most stands erect and free, open to the grace he cannot reach with unaided vision and quite unable to reach that far, unless further aided by God's special grace. Still, Aquinas vindicates the goodness, authenticity, and nobility of the humans God created in his image.

This is the proudest boast of the Catholic intellectual tradition: through Thomas Aquinas, it legitimated, within a Christian vision, all that is good about human nature and its strivings. (Without this, it would be hard to imagine the artistic heritage of Rome.) This Christian humanism, "integral humanism" as Jacques Maritain called it in his famous and influential book just before World War II,[3] is by no means blind to the weakness, sinfulness, and full capacities for evil in the human breast. This humanism nonetheless shares in the satisfaction the Creator took in his creation and, especially, his most beloved creature, man. The most realistic humanism, without illusions, it is quite resolute against nostalgia about the past or utopianism about the future. And it may also be the humanism least closed to the transcendent and most aware of the judgment of God. But humanism it most assuredly is.

The achievement of such a humanism is the first sense in which it is legitimate to speak of Thomas Aquinas as "the first Whig."

The First Whig

In defining the term "Whig" for his own purposes, Friedrich von Hayek proposes a triple test. First, Whigs are the party of liberty. For them, the key to the history of humankind is human liberty. Thus, for example, Lord Acton himself, in praising the early stirrings of the quest for liberty among the nobles gathered around Simon de Montfort, points out that their struggles against the monarch were more clearly articulated by a young scholar of the Order of Preachers in faraway Italy.[4] Liberty, then, is the first theme.

Second, Whigs are thinkers who recognize that their forefathers were at least as bright and serious as they. Whigs guard their patrimony lovingly ("Tradition," Chesterton said, "is the democracy of the dead"). Whigs value the tacit learning and practical originality that accumulates down the ages from the experiments of preceding generations and deeply respect the slow, partial, but organic learning that comes from trial and error. Whigs, in short—by contrast with utopians, revolutionaries, "theoretic politicians" (as James Madison called them),[5] and ideologues (in the original nineteenth-century sense)—place considerable weight on the lessons of experience, on things tried and proved, on tradition, on community, and on values learned organically, implicitly, and often below the level of verbal articulation. This characteristic, more than any other, distinguishes Whigs from "progressives" who are bewitched by bright and new ideas: liberty first and then tradition.

Third, Whigs are thinkers who love existents more than essences. Whigs recognize that, by the laws of human action, human beings must bring into existence what does not yet exist. Whigs welcome this challenge to create, to venture, to act even in the midst of doubts, uncertainties, and mere probabilities. This characteristic most clearly distinguishes Whigs from traditionalists or, as today's fashion has it, paleoconservatives: the Whig theory of action focuses upon the future. Unlike the ancient Greeks, and accepting a lesson from Judaism and Christianity, the Whigs believe that it is the human vocation to construct—patiently and slowly—better institutions for the future: not quite to constitute a better future, however, since Whigs do not expect that human nature changes, but better *institutions* for the future. That is, Whigs hope to create institutions more consonant with the dignity of free men and women.

If they did not believe in slow human progress, Whigs would have to believe that human nature renders men impervious to the lessons of the past, incapable of imagination, and incompetent to nudge human institutions toward more tolerable practices. As they are the party of liberty and tradition, Whigs are also the party of hope—of realistic hope, a modest hope, a carefully checked and balanced hope; they are certainly not the party of fatalism nor the party of nostalgia for some lost golden age.

In short, the Whigs are the party of liberty, tradition, and modest progress. Yet, as Hayek argues so poignantly,[6] to call oneself "progressive" these days is to be enrolled against one's will under a banner that is the euphemism given by the Left to sinister dreams of domination. By comparison with the progressives of today's Left, the Whigs have too much respect for tradition to fall into neodoxy, the doctrine that the unproved new is better. Still, on their other flank, believing in the free polity, the free economy, and the moral and cultural ideal of ordered freedom, contemporary Whigs can scarcely call themselves (in the colloquial sense) "conservatives"; the free society is always, under the inspiration of liberty, open to creativity. Thus, their conservatism is tempered by the desire to test new spirits, to prove the good results of experiments, and—even when experimenting—to provide many checks and balances against abiding tendencies to self-aggrandizement.

Thomas Jefferson once wrote that, on this side of the water, nearly all leading thinkers were Whigs.[7] Indeed, one of the great hymns to the balance between hope and experience sought by true Whigs was given by James Madison in *Federalist* 14, in which, poignantly aware of the novelty of the new American Constitution, he also chooses to recall its deference to sound lessons learned from the past:

> Is it not the glory of the people of America that, whilst they have paid a decent regard to the opinions of former times and other nations, they have not suffered a blind veneration for antiquity, for custom, or for names, to overrule the suggestions of their own good sense, the knowledge of their own situation, and the lessons of their own experience? To this manly spirit posterity will be indebted for the possession, and the world for the example, of the numerous innovations displayed on the American theater in favor of private rights and public happiness.[8]

Now, in these three senses—his commitment to liberty, his love for tradition, and his sense of realistic hope and modest progress— was St. Thomas Aquinas a Whig? No one reading his work can fail to be struck by his zeal to vindicate these three principles. But these are general principles, matters of viewpoint and orientation. The particular case needing additional proof is that his political vision laid down specific practical principles that were to be useful to later generations of Whigs, in the construction of new institutions of political liberty. To these arguments I now turn.

The Civilization of Liberty

It is, of course, misleading to treat a historical figure outside his context. By no means would it be legitimate to ask if Thomas Aquinas were a Whig in the same sense as Thomas Jefferson, James Madison, Edmund Burke, Adam Smith, Lord Acton, or Friedrich von Hayek. The more exact question is, What did Thomas Aquinas hold that might embolden those who today cherish the Whig tradition to count him in their number? There are six propositions of Aquinas that seem particularly compelling to the Whig temper.

First Thesis: Civilization is constituted by reasoned conversation. Two of the most distinguished Thomists of our time, Thomas Gilby, O.P., and John Courtney Murray, S.J., offer the following summary of Aquinas: "Civilization is formed by men locked together in argument. From this dialogue the community becomes a political community."[9] For Aquinas, the most decisive human trait is that human beings are truth-seeking animals, moved by love for the truth (come what may), able to gain insight into complex matters and contingent circumstances, to test hypotheses, and to come to virtually unconditional judgments concerning which hypotheses are true and which are not. So inherent in human nature is this imperative—this drive for understanding, this relentless urge to inquire—that to address a human being in any lesser mode is to do violence to his nature. "The political community," writes Aquinas, "is the sovereign construction of reason." And he elaborates thus:

> Rational creatures are governed for their own benefit, whereas other creatures are governed for the sake of men. Men are principals, not merely instruments.[10]

Humans, therefore, ought to be addressed as free, reasoning, inquiring animals. They ought to be moved by rational persuasion, not by force—and not by demagogy or seduction, either. (Aquinas knew about seduction; to dissuade him from taking a vow of chastity, his own brothers once hired a prostitute and sent her naked into the room where the young man was staying alone. It may not speak well of him in all quarters today, but in this one case, Aquinas did jump to something other than rational persuasion; he drove her out by picking up a hot stick from the fireplace. This suggests to me that he was tempted.)

In a word, that regime is the more civilized which relies less on coercion and more on rational persuasion.[11] This principle of reasoned conversation is probably the one that moved Lord Acton to his original exclamation about "the first Whig."

Not so incidentally, here following Aristotle, Aquinas also recommended that the human mind adopt a "democratic" regime in ruling its own human passions. Neither Aquinas nor Aristotle approved of Plato's image of the mind driving the passions as a charioteer drives his charging steeds. They thought the passions should be treated by the mind as a father reasons with grown sons, not as he would command slaves or servants. The passions deserve to be heard, although not always to be followed. Educated into good habits, under the sweet sway of temperate reason, human passions and sentiments should be neither allowed to be unruly nor brutally suppressed. How civilized a man is shows from the degree to which his passions have been rationally persuaded to follow the urgings of his mind.[12] Nobody ever said that Whigs lacked high ideals.

Second Thesis: The human being is free because he can reflect and choose. Consider the sentence: "The God who gave us life gave us liberty." The words are Thomas Jefferson's, but the thesis is that of Thomas Aquinas. For Aquinas, man is the glory of the universe, an image of God on earth, made to be like God in his liberty.[13] Aquinas contrasted human with other forms of life observable on earth. Inanimate objects are free to be moved, as stones may be moved, but by laws of motion not internal to their being. Vegetative life—oak trees, flowers, tomatoes—have an internal principle of movement; they grow, but their rootedness confines their movement rather narrowly. Animals have an inner principle of movement and freedom of location; they move about, seeking the fulfillment of their sensual and emotional appetites. But human animals have yet another kind of internal principle: their freedom to reflect and to choose among ends proposed to them and among means to reach those ends. Thus Saint Thomas writes:

> A special rule [of Divine providence] applies where intelligent creatures are involved. For they excel all others in the perfection of their nature and the dignity of their end: they are masters of their activity and act freely, while others are more acted on than acting.[14]

In these two capacities, to reflect and to choose, humans are most fittingly called "created in the image of God." No one, of course, sees God. But, as revealed in the Jewish and Christian testaments, the God of the Bible (whom we can neither see with our senses nor imagine in our fantasies) has the capacity to understand and to choose. In creating an image of himself, God made creatures who pursue understanding and who choose. For Aquinas, the work of Aristotle was sufficient proof that one does not have to be a Jew or a Christian to figure this out from the image created, even if one knows nothing of the Creator. The glory of this creation—the human being—was made to be free, therefore responsible, therefore worthy of respect: *dignus*.

Third Thesis: Civilized political institutions respect reflection and choice. In the middle fifty years of the thirteenth century, to speak of democratic republics in the modern sense was to describe no existing regime. And Aquinas was no utopian. Yet just as the well-ordered mind rules human passions "democratically" and not "tyrannically," so monarchs can be judged by the degree to which their regimes rule their subjects tyrannically or through their consent, if only implicit.[15] To argue that Aquinas, before Montesquieu and Madison, foretold the shape of the practical institutions that might allow for the routine and regular expression of such consent by the governed would be to overreach. Nonetheless, St. Thomas validated the search for such institutions. He announced their first principles. He insisted upon their proper measure: the more worthy institutions are of the human person's capacity to reflect and to choose the more civilized they are. If institutions violate that capacity, they are by that much deformed.

We can also go a little further than that. Aquinas established certain limits beyond which governing agents (monarchs) could not go. They are bound by the laws of human nature itself, by the law in man's being that flows directly from God's eternal creative act, by the image of God impressed on man's being. Aquinas did not yet speak of inalienable rights. But he did speak of indelible laws in man's being that command the respect of all, agencies of the state included. No doubt, in a world so marked by disorder as Italy, France, and Germany in the thirteenth century—so characterized by massive fortresses around every tiny island of civilization—Aquinas was duly impressed by the first imperative of civilization, the establishment of the order of law. In his eyes, this meant a government by rulers under law, a law superior to themselves, or in modern terminology "the rule of law, not of men." He saw clearly enough that positive laws, laws framed by legitimate governments, represent practical approximate reflections concerning how *hic et nunc* (here and now) the natural law is to be expressed in particular circumstances. Positive law, to that extent, is worthy of respect and obedience.

Nonetheless, positive laws at variance with man's nature—at variance with the laws of nature and of nature's God—could and should be overturned; their authority is flimsy and ultimately unfounded. Given the rampant disorder of the era, Aquinas could hardly have been a preacher of revolutionary chaos, let alone anarchy. Nonetheless, he did justify, when abuses were flagrant enough and real probabilities of a better order were present, the overthrow of tyrants.[16] For Aquinas, the foundation of law is the human capacity for reflection and choice: man's reasoning nature. On the one hand, to violate that capacity in the name of law is to empty law of its inherent claim to respect and obedience. On the other hand, civilized life demands order. Without authority, common life falls into listlessness, an incapacity for community action, and ultimately chaos. Order there must be, but not just any kind of order. Only a reasonable order does justice to the dignity of citizens. Unlike the moderns, Aquinas does not argue from the violence of lack of order (although that argument is not unknown to him), so much as from the human propensity for reasoned conversation in community.

Fourth Thesis: True liberty is ordered liberty. The glory of the human being is personal liberty: that is, the liberty to choose from reflection and due deliberation. To choose merely by whim or desire or inclination, without reflection, is to live as other animals do. Among the creatures of this earth, observably, humans have a unique power to choose. Just as visibly, humans do not always develop this power and do not always exercise it. To develop this special liberty from potency to active exercise requires the ability to maintain a sense of responsibility even in the heat of events. This ability, in turn, depends upon a full panoply of those "manly strengths" (virtues) possessed by great warriors: calmness and clear vision in the battle, command of the passions, a sense of proportion, and correctives against personal weaknesses. Often passion grips us, or lethargy, or the turmoil of contrary inclinations. To place all these under the sway of reason requires habits that protect our capacities for reflection and decision from being overwhelmed.[17] Temperance, fortitude, a sense of proportion (justice), and practical wisdom are the names given to these four central settled dispositions, which are characteristic of the person whose capacities for reflection and decision are unimpeded from within. These cardinal habits give order to our capacity for human freedom. They are not easy to develop; they are partly a gift and partly earned by repeated effort. Thus, the conquest of personal liberty requires self-education in the virtues necessary to ordered liberty: no such habits, no actual liberty.

The proudest boast of the young Whig republic, the United States, was the legendary manly strength (virtue) of its leaders, notably George Washington, James Madison, and Thomas Jefferson— and also the virtue of its people, who were asked in an unprecedented way to reflect and to deliberate upon the ratification of the Constitution under which they would live and to maintain sufficient virtue to keep the republic from the self-destruction into which all earlier republics had speedily fallen.

Fifth Thesis: Humans are self-determined persons, not mere individuals (group members). As an *individual*, a citizen is only part of a whole and in this aspect may be asked, for sufficient reason, to lay down his or her life for the whole. As a *person*, a citizen is an autonomous subject who participates in the liberty proper to the Creator and is thus an end in himself—an end for which the world was created, more valuable than the world. By shifting attention from the individual (mere member of a collective) to the person (self-determining, an end and not a means), Aquinas reached the conclusion that the internal capacities of the person transcend the purposes and limited powers of the state. From a purely philosophical point of view, each person has a responsibility to direct his own destiny. From a theological point of view (Jewish and Christian), each person has been created to share in the life of God.

"In human affairs," writes St. Thomas, "there is the common good, the well-being of the state or nation; there is also a human good which does not lie in the community, but is personal to each man in himself."[18] And in the *Summa Theologica*, he says: "Person signifies what is noblest in the whole of nature,"[19] and again,

> Men are principals, not merely instruments. . . . Providence directs rational creatures for the welfare and growth of the individual person, not just for the advantage of the race. . . . Actions have a personal value, and are not merely from and for human nature. . . . The intent of the divine law given to man is to lead him to God. The will cleaves to another either from love or from fear. But there is a great difference between these motives. In the case of fear the first consideration is not the loved object itself but something else, namely, the evil that would impend but for its presence. In the case of love the union is sought for the very sake of the beloved. What is for its own sake is more primary than what is for an outside reason. Hence, love is our strongest union with God, and this above all is intended by the divine law. The entire purpose of the lawgiver is that man may love God.[20]

In the Jewish and Christian view, humans are made for far more than the purposes of the state or even of the whole of civil society in this world. No matter how powerful or how rich a society might become, and no matter how famous, successful, or wealthy a person may become, each person has been made to be restless until he rests in God, and each society stands under God's judgment. No state or no law is legitimate that blocks the free exercise of this quest for God.

Sixth Thesis: The regime worthiest of the human person mixes elements of monarchy, aristocracy, and democracy. According to historical experience up to the mid-thirteenth century, each of the three main types of regime so far known to history—monarchical, aristocratic, and democratic—had such grievous faults that the best regime, worthiest of human persons, would seem to be a regime that combines the best elements of all three. Aquinas did not invent this typology of regimes; he borrowed it from Aristotle and Cicero but gave it his own grounding and exposition. Every human person, given the capacities for personal responsibility, ought to participate responsibly in forming a worthy regime. Regimes gain their authority from the practical wisdom they embody, a wisdom participated in by every citizen. Thus, the justness of regimes is measured by human reason. Regimes ought, threrefore, to be based on the consent of citizens. (Indeed, the fact of dissension explains why tyrannies, odious to many, are not likely to be of long duration.)[21] Rule by one strong leader is best but is so easily corrupted into tyranny, the worst form of government, that it requires remedies. A virtuous aristocracy may check a strong leader and help to maintain him, if not in virtue, at least in wise pursuit of the common good, rather than in personal aggrandizement. Legitimacy comes from the participation of all citizens in choosing their leader (and perhaps in rotating him at regular intervals). Here it is best to let Aquinas speak for himself:

> Two points should be observed concerning the healthy constitution of a state or nation. One is that all should play a responsible part in the governing: this ensures peace, and the arrangement is liked and maintained by all. The other concerns the type of government; on this head the best arrangement for a state or government is for one to be placed in command, presiding by authority over all, while under him are others with administrative powers, yet for the rulers to belong to all because they are elected by and from all. Such is the best polity, well combined from the different strains of monarchy, since there is one at the head; of aristocracy, since many are given responsibility; and of democracy, since the rulers are chosen from and by the people.[22]

In summary, the six theses are:
• Civilization is reasoned conversation.
• The human being is free because he can reflect and choose.
• Civilized political institutions respect reflection and choice.
• True liberty is ordered liberty.
• Humans are self-determined persons, not mere individuals or group members.
• To guard against abuses, the regime worthiest of the human person mixes elements of monarchy, aristocracy, and democracy.

A Whig in Principle, Not in Institutional Detail

These six theses of St. Thomas Aquinas, to which others might be added and much more detail on each appended, would seem to justify the willingness of Lord Acton and Friedrich von Hayek to call Aquinas "the first Whig." Each of these theses echoes throughout subsequent history. They also indicate much work yet to be done, including philosophical (and theological) efforts to clarify the intellectual foundations of today's free societies. This also includes much practical work to shape our social institutions so that such principles may more thoroughly suffuse them, rendering them more humane, reasonable, and self-correcting.

Nonetheless, in the actual course of Western history, in the great historical experiments that led to our modern liberal societies, direct intellectual links with these six theses of Aquinas were broken. Aquinas was not much read, if at all, by Hobbes, Montesquieu, Locke, Rousseau, or others who played so large a role on the stage of political philosophy in the past three centuries. This rupture has had many deleterious consequences for our culture. For one thing, the Enlightenment project in ethics—to establish an ethic based on modern conceptions of reason—today lies in ruins.[23] For another, the split between secular philosophy and religion has marooned the majority of churchgoers and isolated the academics and the intellectuals.[24] These severe rifts in our culture do not bode well for our cultural integrity.

Furthermore, it would be quite wrong to overlook the large gap that yawns between the articulation of basic *principles* in Aquinas and the discovery of *institutions* that actually incarnate these principles in practice. As Aquinas himself remarked in his *Commentary on Aristotle's Politics:* "Practical science differs from theoretical science in that it is meant to work." For this reason, he lists political science among the practical sciences: "The political community is a group which the reason *shapes* as well as discusses" (emphasis added).[25] This sort of philosophy is meant to work, not merely to be admired in idle elegance.

The modern Whigs went far beyond Aquinas in making political philosophy work. It was not Aquinas who imagined that the powers of the executive and the legislature should be limited and framed by constitutional law, interpreted by an independent judiciary. It was not Aquinas who imagined practical methods of reconciling "energy in the executive" with an "aristocratic" Senate and a "democratic" House of Representatives. It was not Aquinas who first thought of the separation of powers. It was not Aquinas who first articulated the even more fundamental separation of *systems:* the limited state, flanked on one side by the larger moral-cultural system (composed of such basic institutions as free churches, a free press, and free cultural associations of many sorts) and on the other side by a free economy.

In particular, Aquinas never studied economic history; and this remains a great task looming before Thomistic thought. Both historical experience and his own concept of the free person had early persuaded Aquinas of the practical necessity of a regime of private property. But his own skepticism about money, money making, and free markets mark Aquinas as no early progenitor of capitalism. In his day, most wealth was gained by plunder or conquest or favors from kings and emperors, not from commerce or manufacture or invention. He never lived to see the great economic transformation of modern times. To have seen it might have strengthened his esteem for practical intelligence, because it is the source of the ultimate form of capital.

Nonetheless, in political philosophy, Aquinas provided a justification for and honored what the later Whigs would take up as their supreme vocation. "The political community," Aquinas wrote, "is the sovereign construction of reason," specifically of practical reason: "So political science must needs be the chief and governing practical interest, since it is occupied with the most final and complete value within the present world." Political philosophy "rounds off the philosophy of human nature."[26] Political philosophy is less important, Aquinas thinks, than the study of God, who is the end citizens and polities obscurely seek. Political philosophy is under God's judgment. Nonetheless, political philosophy is, of all inquiries within the present order, the most noble. Thus did Aquinas pay his successor Whigs high honor and confirm their nobility.

In calling Aquinas with propriety the first Whig, therefore, it would be wrong to derogate from the full, practical originality of the Whigs who appeared in history some four or more centuries later than he did. They had plenty to invent and to achieve on their own. So it would not do to give Aquinas more credit than he deserves—or less. He helped to establish, and to justify in the Christian world, the Whig values of liberty, tradition, and institutional progress. He paid high honor to the political vocation. He held together concepts that many later thinkers treated as dichotomies—concepts such as freedom and order, person and community, knowledge through the senses and intelligence, passion and virtue, tradition and progress, the evil in man and the good, nature and grace, faith and inquiry. On each of these matters, he may have been the deepest thinker in the Whig tradition. In trying to deepen the intellectual formulations of that tradition, and in particular to build a bridge between the philosophical and the religious ways of addressing questions of liberty, one could do worse than to seek some fresh starting points in Aquinas. Liberty, tradition, institutional progress—all three Whig principles rest on deep formulations in his work.

Toward the Future

Indeed, several basic concepts of Aquinas are experiencing a very strong revival today and are likely to become yet more powerful in the future. First among these are the ideas of character and virtue. James Q. Wilson has remarked that the greatest intellectual event of the past twenty years has been a revival of the concept of "character."[27] In the work of Alasdair MacIntyre, Stanley Hauerwas, and James Gustafson, the same may be said of those virtues that for Aquinas and Aristotle are the chief protectors of human liberty in practice.[28] Apart from the exercise of virtue and character, in fact, it would seem that human liberty is little more than a cloud of whimsy, desire, and inclination, which reflective reason, like the lamp of Lady Liberty, has yet to dispel.

Second, as this planet's 165 or so nations become ever more interdependent, the much ballyhooed cultural relativism of recent generations comes under closer universal, planetary moral standards. If it is immoral to practice torture in Argentina, then it is also immoral in Uganda, Syria, and the People's Republic of China. If citizens of Hungary and Poland claim inalienable rights and break the power monopoly of the Communist party, then the Baltic nations and Ukraine, Armenia, and other republics have the right to do the same. In such fashion, the horrible abuses of the human person in the twentieth century have led to the gradual emergence of a virtually universal condemnation of certain practices.

These condemnations may yet fall far short of practical effect, from want of regular and routine systems that enforce the declared standards of behavior. Nonetheless, the principles of what might be called a universal natural law, binding upon all members of our species (whether they like it or not), seem to be attracting a dim but sure consensus. Perhaps, as if in confirmation of Aquinas, Cicero, and Aristotle, the dotted lines of what one day may be recognized as the natural law of a species that respects its own capacities for ordered liberty are emerging, waiting to be fully adumbrated both in human consciousness and in institutions that work.

Third, from one point of view, the so-called environmental crisis seems to have tempered the arrogant claim of the Enlightenment that knowledge is power, that is, *merely* power. Nor is knowledge merely a way to distance oneself from all things, as an objective observer. Knowledge is, first of all, truth. It is a learned respect for reality and indeed for the interaction of the knowing subject with the known. Through knowledge, the human soul is called "to become all things" and to live in this world with that ordered knowledge that is wisdom. The environmental crisis calls for a new way of relating knowledge and power, more like that of certain ancients, less like that of the modern rationalists. But this is to call not for less knowledge, but more—not for irrationality and nostalgia, but for a deeper and wiser ordering of human affairs.

From another point of view, however, ecological consciousness today displays all the hallmarks of a gnostic religion. As if we had witnessed the death of the real God, Mother Nature herself has now been set up as an idol. To her, calculating priests minister, the gurus of grim. Before her, the poor of this world are expected to grovel, since economic growth must be sacrificed at her altars.[29] Moreover, this Mother Nature is now prettified with cosmetics. It is forgotten that down through history she has exercised, in earthquake and hurricane, plague and drought, pestilential wind and poisonous water, a bitter threat to human survival. This goddess of the new fundamentalism has taken millions of infants in childbirth, wiped out whole cities with smallpox, infiltrated consuming tapeworms into the bellies of children in the jungles, and for most of human history has cut down with her scythe so many so recklessly as to keep the average age of human death below eighteen. In the face of this new fundamentalism, the Whig task is, as it has always been, to defend liberty, to learn from trial and error, and to make solid institutional progress.

It was, after all, on a note of doom and damnation that the early Middle Ages began; and it was the role of the first Whig to calm fevered passions. As Thomas Gilby remarks: "Iconography shows St. Thomas calm and sedate, a book on his lap, his fingers expository; he is not proclaiming, denouncing, or wringing his hands. He was singularly free from the homilist's complaint of living in bad times."[30]

The Whig task in history is by no means at an end. The construction of institutions worthy of free men and women—a construction that is sovereign among the practical sciences—will never end. In the thirteenth century when Aquinas thought that the human pilgrimage was an adventure with much remaining to be done, he was not wrong. Nor will we be. "Person signifies what is noblest in the whole of nature," Aquinas wrote.[31] And Maritain glosses yet another of his texts: "By its liberty, the human person transcends the stars and all the world of nature."[32] These are Whig sentiments, worth keeping alive in yet another generation to pass on to the next.

Notes

Chapter 1: Introduction—Building Bridges

1. A useful anthology describing the Catholic underpinnings of the social and political thought of southern Europe and Latin America is Howard J. Wiarda, ed., *Politics and Social Change in Latin America: The Distinct Tradition* 3rd ed. (Boulder, Colo.: Westview Press, 1991).

Chapter 2: Reconstituting a Social Order

1. G. M. Tamas, "High and Dry, East and West," *The Spectator*, December 10, 1988, p. 17.

2. Thomas Jefferson to Henry Lee, May 8, 1825, in Adrienne Koch and William Peden, eds., *The Life and Selected Writings of Thomas Jefferson* (New York: Modern Library, 1944), p. 719.

3. See Encyclical *Sollicitudo Rei Socialis*, p. 33.

4. See the pope's speeches in Chile, printed in *Estudios Publicos*, no. 26, Otono 1987.

5. Friedrich von Hayek, *The Constitution of Liberty* (Chicago: Henry Regnery, 1960), p. 457, n. 4.

6. *Origins*, vol. 24, September 1987.

7. See Michael Novak, "Narrative and Ideology," *This World*, vol. 23 (Fall 1988), pp. 66–80.

8. See Walter Berns, *Taking the Constitution Seriously* (New York: Simon and Schuster, 1987), "The Commercial Republic," pp. 173–76; and Ralph Lerner, *The Thinking Revolutionary* (Ithaca, N.Y.: Cornell University Press, 1987), chap. 6, "Commerce and Character."

9. See Adam Smith, *An Inquiry into the Nature and Causes of the Wealth of Nations*, ed. R. H. Campbell and A. S. Skinner (Indianapolis: Liberty Press, 1976), p. 145.

10. Thomas Jefferson to Thomas Mann Randolph, May 30, 1790, in Koch and Peden, eds., *Life and Selected Writings of Thomas Jefferson*, pp. 496–97.

11. J. Hector St. John Crevecoeur, *Letters from an American Farmer* (1782; reprint, New York: Fox, Duffield & Co., 1904), p. 55.

12. "The Americans," writes Alexis de Tocqueville, "enjoy explaining almost every act of their lives on the principle of self-interest properly understood. It gives them pleasure to point out how an enlightened self-love continually leads them to help one another and disposes them freely to give part of their time and wealth for the good of the state" (*Democracy in America*,

George Lawrence, trans., and J. P. Mayer, ed. [Garden City, N.Y.: Doubleday & Company, Inc., 1969], p. 526).

CHAPTER 3: PRIORITY OF COMMUNITY, PRIORITY OF PERSONS

1. Aristotle, *Nicomachean Ethics,* in *The Basic Works of Aristotle,* edited with an introduction by Richard McKeon (New York: Random House, 1941), bk. 10, chap. 9 (1179b19).

2. See Michael Novak, "Estructuras de Virtud, Estructuras de Pecado," in *Estudios Publicos,* no. 31 (Invierno 1988), pp. 231–46; the English version appeared in *America,* January 28, 1989, pp. 54–60.

3. See Wilhelm Windelband, *A History of Philosophy,* vol. 1 (New York: Greenwood, 1958), p. 257; compare also Franz Mueller, "Person and Society according to St. Thomas Aquinas," *Aquin Papers* (St. Paul, Minn.: College of St. Thomas, n.d.), no. 17, preface.

4. Franz Mueller argues that "there are essentially different reasons for the living together of gregarious animals and that of men." The difference can be traced to man's "personal" as distinguished from his "individual" nature, and man's "personal nature exists only secondarily for the sake of the human race, but primarily for his own sake." It follows that, although St. Thomas "proclaims the primacy of the common weal [over the particular], he confirms at the same time the existence of an individual good and its relative autonomy in its own sphere. 'There is a certain good proper to every man insofar as he is a single person. . . .

There is, on the other hand, another, the common good, which pertains to this one or that one as far as they are parts of some whole, as to the soldier insofar as he is a part of the army, and to the citizen in so far as he is a part of the state,' " see ibid., pp. 21, 26. Similarly, Jacques Maritain writes that

> it is the human person who enters into society; as an individual, he enters society as a part whose proper good is inferior to the good of the whole (of the whole constituted of persons). But the good of the whole is what it is, and is therefore superior to the private good, only if it benefits the individual persons, is redistributed to them, and respects their dignity (*The Social and Political Philosophy of Jacques Maritain* [New York: Charles Scribner's Sons, 1955], p. 87).

5. Thus St. Thomas quotes this passage from Aristotle, *Nicomachean Ethics,* book 1, chap. 2 (1094b). E. Kurz, O.F.M., has counted the occurrences of this passage in St. Thomas; see *Individuum und Gemeinschaft beim Hl. Thomas v. Acquin* (Munich: 1933), p. 47.

6. Thomas Aquinas only reluctantly found reasons for calling a war "just." He phrased his question in the negative: "Can war ever be just?" *Summa Theologica,* II.II, Q XL.

7. Lord Acton gave Aquinas credit for this theory in "The History of Freedom in Christianity," *Essays on Freedom and Power,* ed. Gertrude Himmelfarb (New York: World Publishing Co., 1955), p. 88. He writes that the language found in the "earliest exposition of the Whig theory of the revolution, is taken from the works of St. Thomas Aquinas. . . ."

8. In the very first paragraph of *The Federalist*, Alexander Hamilton called attention to the centrality of reflection and choice:

> It has been frequently remarked that it seems to have been reserved to the people of this country, by their conduct and example, to decide the important question, whether societies of men are really capable or not of establishing good government from *reflection* and *choice*, or whether they are forever destined to depend for their political constitutions on accident and force (*The Federalist Papers*, intro. by Clinton Rossiter [New York: New American Library of World Literature, 1961], p. 33 [italics added]).

9. If patient observation and sincere meditation have led men of the present day to recognize that both the past and the future of their history consist in the gradual and measured advance of equality, that discovery in itself gives this progress the sacred character of the will of the Sovereign Master. In that case effort to halt democracy appears as a fight against God Himself, and nations have no alternative but to acquiesce in the social state imposed by Providence (Alexis de Tocqueville, *Democracy in America*, trans. George Lawrence, ed. J. P. Mayer [Garden City, N.Y.: Doubleday & Company, Inc., 1969], p. 12).

10. Ibid., p. 514; see also p. 189: "Better use has been made of assocation and this powerful instrument of action has been applied to more varied aims in America than anywhere else in the world."

11. Ibid., p. 513.

12. Ibid., p. 517. "It cannot be repeated too often," Tocqueville writes, that "nothing is more fertile in marvels than the art of being free, but nothing is harder than freedom's apprenticeship" (p. 240). Especially in ages of democracy, the defense of freedom requires an arduous education. "A great deal of intelligence, knowledge, and skill are required in these circumstances to organize and maintain secondary powers and to create, among independent but individually weak citizens, free associations which can resist tyranny without destroying public order" (p. 676).

13. See note 17 below.

14. See Peter L. Berger and Richard John Neuhaus, *To Empower People* (Washington, D.C.: American Enterprise Institute, 1977), chap. 5, "Voluntary Association."

15. "The State," writes Maritain in *Man and the State*, "is neither a whole nor a subject of right, or a person. It is a part of the body politic, and, as such, inferior to the body politic as a whole, subordinate to it, and at the service of its common good. The common good of the political society is the final aim of the State, and comes before the immediate aim of the State"(Chicago: University of Chicago Press, 1951), p. 24. For a more detailed account see "The People and the State," chap. 1 in *Man and the State*, pp. 1–27.

16. Franz Mueller writes:

> Precisely because man is a person and because in his consciousness and in his conscience, he can, as it were, converse with himself, he seeks to communicate with others in the order of knowledge and

love. Such intercommunication wherein man really gives himself
and wherein he is really received is something without which the
human person cannot achieve perfection. The spiritual soul, the
likeness of God in man, would be stunted without such communication.

Thus, Mueller concludes, "man requires the assistance of his fellow men,
not primarily because he has been deprived of parts and powers which he
needs to be a complete substance, or even because he was created a helpless
being, but because it is natural for him to tend toward communion" ("Person
and Society," p. 20).

17. Following Tocqueville, Hannah Arendt notes a crucial distinction between a people and a mob. A mob is approached through the stampeding of
its passions, as through a demagogue. A mob is but a collection of individuals, animated not by their autonomous capacities for making choices
through reflection and reasoned discourse, but rather by their unformed
passions swayed by whatever winds may blow. By contrast, a people is an
assembly of many smaller assemblies, each with its own forms of reasoned
association and reflective consent. A people is a large society of many smaller
societies, within which reason holds sway. Thus, Arendt observed a crucial
difference between the social condition of North Americans and the social
condition of the populations of Europe (France in particular). In America,
she noted, there was a people; in France, the masses and the mob. The
people of North America had had the good fortune, as Tocqueville had
noted, to organize themselves first in villages and other local communities;
then in townships; then in counties; then in states; and, only after the
passage of 150 years, in a national, federal government. By this time they
were neither a mass nor a mob but a people—and, after their consent to the
Constitution of 1776, a sovereign people. See Hannah Arendt, *On Revolution*
(New York: Viking Press, 1965), pp. 69–73, 88–90, 274; and Tocqueville,
Democracy in America, "The Need to Study What Happens in the States before
Discussing the Government of the Union," pp. 61–98.

18. Father J. Miquel Ibanez Langlois, for example, made such a charge
against Paul Johnson and me in *El Mercurio* (Santiago, Chile), September
1988, p. E6. Gonzalo Rojas Sanches responded on our behalf in the same
pages (October 23, 1988), p. E15.

19. Jacques Maritain, *Reflections on America* (New York: Charles Scribner's
Sons, 1958).

20. Thomas Jefferson, "A Summary View of the Rights of British America,
1774," in Adrienne Koch and William Peden, eds., *The Life and Selected
Writings of Thomas Jefferson* (New York: Modern Library, 1972), p. 311.

CHAPTER 4: THE VIRTUE OF ENTERPRISE

1. For two introductions to Adam Smith, see Irving Kristol, *Reflections of a
Neoconservative* (New York: Basic Books, 1983), chap. 12, "Adam Smith and
the Spirit of Capitalism"; and Gertrude Himmelfarb, *The Idea of Poverty* (New
York: Alfred A. Knopf, 1984), chap. 2, "Adam Smith: Political Economy as
Moral Philosophy."

2. "It will be noticed," writes Mill in his "Preliminary Remarks" to the *Principles of Political Economy*, "that political economy does not include ethics, legislation, or the science of government." He immediately adds, however, that "the results of political economy are offered to the statesman, who reaches a conclusion after weighing them in connection with moral and political considerations." *The Principles of Political Economy*, abridged, with critical, bibliographical, and explanatory notes, by J. Laurence Laughlin (New York: D. Appleton and Company, 1888), p. 47.

3. On this point, Pesch wrote that "morally advanced peoples will, no doubt, profit economically from the active, especially the social, virtues of their citizens and will be better prepared to endure physical evil and hard times." He is aware, of course, that "this does not mean that the economist should theologize or moralize in the treatment of his subject matter or, what is worse, try to derive an economic system from Holy Scripture." Quoted in Franz Mueller, "I knew Heinrich Pesch," *Social Order*, vol. 1, no. 4 (April 1951), p. 151. See also my discussion of Pesch in *Freedom with Justice: Catholic Social Thought and Liberal Institutions* (San Francisco: Harper & Row, 1984), pp. 69–80.

4. See Thomas Sowell, *The Economics and Politics of Race: An International Perspective* (New York: William Morrow and Co., Inc., 1983); in the American context, see also his *Ethnic America* (New York: Basic Books, 1981), chap. 1, "The American Mosaic."

5. Since the early centuries of Christianity, the fathers of the Church, bishops and theologians have repeatedly pointed out that God, in His goodness, has distributed natural resources and the agricultural products unevenly among the various countries in order to stimulate nations to friendly exchange and to link them together in a peaceful manner. Saint John Chrysostom (who died in 407) argued that it is God's will that not everything can grow and be produced everywhere on earth so as to link peoples closely together by an exchange of goods. . . . Heinrich Heinbuche von Langenstein (born in Hesse in 1325) took up this line of thought and argued that the task of foreign trade lay in joining together nations 'in friendship and love.' John Mayr, a Scotsman (died in 1550), observed that no country can exist without commerce (Joseph Cardinal Hoeffner, "The World Economy in the Light of Catholic Social Teaching," in Lothar Roos, ed., *Ordo Socialis*, May 1987, pp. 26–27).

6. See I Corinthians 12:12–26:

The body is one and has many members, but all the members, many though they are, are one body. . . . Now the body is not one member, it is many. If the foot should say, 'Because I am not a hand I do not belong to the body,' would it then no longer belong to the body? If the ear should say, 'Because I am not an eye I do not belong to the body,' would it then no longer belong to the body? If the body were all eye, what would happen to our hearing? If it were all ear, what would happen to our smelling? As it is, God has set each member of the body in the place he wanted it to be. If all the members were alike, where would the body be? . . . Even those members of the body which seem less important are in fact indispensable. . . . If one member suffers, all the members suffer with it; if one member is honored, all the members share its joy.

7. Adam Smith, *An Inquiry into the Nature and Causes of the Wealth of Nations*, ed. R. H. Campbell and A. S. Skinner (Indianapolis: Liberty Press, 1976), vol. 1, pp. 14–15.

8. See Warren T. Brookes, *The Economy in Mind*, foreword by George Gilder (New York: Universe Books, 1982); Lawrence E. Harrison, *Underdevelopment Is a State of Mind: The Latin American Case* (Boston: Madison Books, 1985); and Julian L. Simon, *The Ultimate Resource* (Princeton: Princeton University Press, 1981). Capitalism is often—but erroneously—defined in terms of private property, markets, and profits. But such definitions cannot be accurate. For the truth is that all these things existed even in the biblical period. Jerusalem in the Bible was a trading center, little more. In Jerusalem were found private property, markets, and profits. Yet no one holds that biblical Jerusalem was a capitalist city. On the contrary, the name *capitalism* was invented to name a new reality, emergent over many generations, but coming to fruition only in about the last decades of the eighteenth century. And what was precisely new about capitalism was its organization around creative intellect: evident in such simple examples as the invention of the pin machine, of the railroad locomotive, of the Singer sewing machine, and of most of the other instruments of daily life today. For the phrase from Adam Smith, see *The Wealth of Nations*, Introduction, vol. 1, pp. 10–11.

9. He was not the first to do this. Heinrich Pesch, one of whose students, Oswald von Nell-Breuning, S.J., was later co-author of Pius XI's *Quadragesimo Anno*, had also written about the link between enterprise and creativity: "We owe to free competitive enterprise the great benefits of the last century in the field of knowledge and 'know-how'; in it dwells a never-failing, animated, creative force; it is able to harness forces for the highest production, always creating new goods for the welfare of the people." Quoted in Richard E. Mulcahy, S.J., "Economic Freedom in Pesch," *Social Order*, vol. 1 (April 1951), p. 163. See also von Nell-Breuning, *Reorganization of Social Economy: The Social Encyclical Developed and Explained* (New York: Bruce Publishing Company, 1936), chap. 6, "Wealth and Commonwealth," especially p. 116.

10. See *Sollicitudo Rei Socialis*, 15, pp. 16–17. For the full text and extended commentary, see Kenneth A. Meyers, ed., *Aspiring to Freedom* (Grand Rapids, Mich.: Erdmans Publishing Co., 1988).

11. "The free institutions and the political rights enjoyed" in America, writes Tocqueville,

provide a thousand continual reminders to every citizen that he lives in society. At every moment they bring his mind back to this idea, that it is the duty as well as the interest of men to be useful to their fellows. Having no particular reason to hate others, since he is neither their slave nor their master, the American's heart easily inclines toward benevolence. At first it is of necessity that men attend to the public interest, afterward by choice. What had been calculation becomes instinct. By dint of working for the good of his fellow citizens, he in the end acquires a habit and taste for serving them (*Democracy in America*, trans. George Lawrence and ed. J. P. Mayer [Garden City, N.Y.: Doubleday & Company, Inc., 1969], pp. 512–13).

12. For two excellent discussions by a contemporary economist, see Israel M. Kirzner, "The Entrepreneur," in *Competition and Entrepreneurship* (Chicago: University of Chicago Press, 1973), pp. 30–87; and "The Primacy of Entrepreneurial Discovery," in *Discovery and the Capitalist Process* (Chicago: University of Chicago Press, 1985), pp. 15–39.

13. See Bernard Murchland, *Humanism and Capitalism: A Survey of Thought on Morality* (Washington, D.C.: American Enterprise Institute, 1984), p. 57. But this humanism, continues Murchland, "is neither perfect nor complete. We need a more integral humanism." He then offers ten principles "for a stronger, more comprehensive humanism"; see pp. 57–62; see also, chap. 3, "Democratic Capitalism: The Other Humanism."

14. Jacques Maritain, *Art and Scholasticism*, trans. Joseph W. Evans (New York: Charles Scribner's Sons, 1962), p. 9.

15. See Michael Novak, "Cash Income and the Family Farm: Reflections on Catholic Theology and the Democratic Capitalist Political Economy of Agriculture" (Lecture delivered at Iowa State University, February 27, 1987).

16. For additional details, see Norman McCrae, "The Next Ages of Man," *The Economist*, December 24, 1988, pp. 6ff. Summarizing a speech by Alan Greenspan, the chairman of the U.S. Federal Reserve Board of Governors, George F. Will writes that "the rapid expansion of international trade is produced in part by technology, particularly the shrinkage of the size of products. . . . Greenspan says the recent improvement in the economic well-being of most nations occurred without significant change in the physical bulk or weight of gross national product." This "decline in the bulk and weight of goods is a result of what Greenspan calls 'the conceptual contribution to economic activity.' " "This Wired World," *Washington Post*, January 5, 1987.

17. See Lester C. Thurow, review of *The Capitalist Revolution*, by Peter L. Berger, "Who Stays Up with the Sick Cow?" *New York Times Book Review*, September 7, 1986.

18. For a discussion of such obstacles in Latin American economies, see Hernando de Soto, *The Other Path: The Invisible Revolution in the Third World*, trans. June Abbott (New York: Harper and Row, 1989).

19. Lord Peter Bauer has called attention to how absurd it is, therefore, to count the birth of a calf or the survival of a cow as an incremental *addition* to a nation's net capital income, while the birth or survival of a child—who, after all, is the source of new creativity—is counted a *diminution* of that income. See *Equality, the Third World and Economic Delusion* (Cambridge, Mass.: Harvard University Press, 1981), p. 21; see also "The Population Explosion: Myths and Realities," ibid., pp. 42–65. In *Reality and Rhetoric: Studies in the Economics of Development* (Cambridge, Mass.: Harvard University Press, 1984), p. 9, Lord Bauer argues that "the relation between economic development and population growth cannot be examined sensibly on the basis simply of numbers and resources."

CHAPTER 5: STRUCTURES OF VIRTUE, STRUCTURES OF SIN

1. In his "Address to the Economic Commission for Latin America and the Caribbean," Santiago, Chile, April 3, 1987, Pope John Paul II emphasized "the priority of maximum employment" in this way:

> Housing, food, health, and other subsidies granted to the poorest man are absolutely essential, but he, we might say, is not the actor in this certainly praiseworthy act of mercy. Whereas to offer him work is to set in motion the essential resource of his human activity whereby the worker becomes possessed of his destiny, becomes part of society as a whole, even receives other forms of aid not as alms but, to some extent, as the living and personal fruit of his own effort.

2. See chap. 4, n. 8. The pope adds that in our "concern for the poor, one must not overlook that *special form of poverty* which consists in being deprived of fundamental human rights, in particular the right to religious freedom and also the right to freedom of economic initiative."

3. Alexander Hamilton, James Madison, and John Jay, *The Federalist Papers* (New York: New American Library, 1961), No. 51, p. 322.

4. June 20, 1788, Virginia Ratifying Convention, in Jonathan Elliot, ed., *Debates in the Several State Conventions on the Adoption of the Federal Constitution* (Philadelphia: Lippincott, 1907).

5. Madison, *Federalist* No. 51, p. 322.

6. U.S. Constitution, Preamble.

7. "It cannot be repeated too often," Tocqueville wrote,

> nothing is more fertile in marvels than the art of being free, but nothing is harder than freedom's apprenticeship. The same is not true of despotism. Despotism often presents itself as the repairer of all the ills suffered, the supporter of just rights, defender of the oppressed, and founder of order. Peoples are lulled to sleep by the temporary prosperity it engenders, and when they do wake up, they are wretched. But liberty is generally born in stormy weather, growing with difficulty amid civil discords, and only when it is already old does one see the blessings it has brought (*Democracy in America*, ed. J. P. Mayer, trans. George Lawrence [Garden City, N.Y.: Doubleday & Company, Inc., 1969], p. 240).

8. See n. 2, above. John Paul II had earlier emphasized the importance of economic initiative in Latin America: "The challenge of poverty is of such magnitude that to overcome it we must resort to the full dynamics and creativeness of private enterprise, to all its potential effectiveness, its capacity for efficient allocation of resources, and the fullness of its renovating energies" (Address to the Economic Commission for Latin America and the Caribbean, Santiago, Chile, April 3, 1987).

9. Only one "right" is specifically mentioned in the original Constitution: "Congress shall have power . . . to promote the progress of science and useful arts, by securing for limited times to authors and inventors the exclusive right to their respective writings and discoveries" (Article I, section 8).

10. See Nathan Rosenberg and L. E. Birdzell, Jr., *How the West Grew Rich: The Economic Transformation of the Industrial World* (New York: Basic Books, 1986).

11. John Paul II concludes *Sollicitudo Rei Socialis* with the theme of liberty:

> Peoples and individuals aspire to be free: their search for full development signals their desire to overcome the many obstacles preventing them from enjoying a 'more human life' . . . the aspiration to freedom from all forms of slavery affecting the individual and society is something *noble* and *legitimate*. This in fact is the purpose of development, or rather liberation and development [emphasis in original].

12. See chap. 4, n. 5.

13. See Alejandro Antonio Chafuen, *Christians for Freedom* (San Francisco, Calif.: Ignatius Press, 1987), esp. chap. 6, "Commerce, Merchants, and Tradesmen": "The exchange of goods with foreign merchants is, for Bartolome de Albornoz, the 'most natural [contract] that exists in humanity.' " Furthermore, he stated that

> Buying and selling is the nerve of human life that sustains the universe. By means of buying and selling the world is united, joining distant lands and nations, people of different languages, laws and ways of life. If it were not for these contracts, some would lack the goods that others have in abundance, and they would not be able to share the goods that they have in excess with those countries where they are scarce (p. 91, quoting Bartolome de Albornoz, *Arte de los Contratos* [Valencia, 1573], chap. 7, p. 29).

14. See Peter Berger, *The Capitalist Revolution* (New York: Basic Books, 1986).

CHAPTER 6: ECONOMIC DEVELOPMENT FROM THE BOTTOM UP

1. In *Laborem Exercens*, Pope John Paul II reiterated Thomas Aquinas's argument:

> The person who works desires not only due remuneration for his work; he also wishes that within the production process provision be made for him to be able to know that in his work, even on something that is owned in common, he is working "for himself." This awareness is extinguished within him in a system of excessive bureaucratic centralization, which makes the worker feel that he is just a cog in a huge machine moved from above. . . . In the mind of St. Thomas Aquinas, this is the principal reason in favor of private ownership of the means of production (no. 15).

2. Alejandro A. Chafuen, "What St. Bernadine's Ass Could Teach the Bishops," *Reason* (August/September 1987), pp. 43–44.

3. Roy P. Basler, ed., *The Collected Works of Abraham Lincoln*, 8 vols. (New Brunswick, N.J.: Rutgers University Press, 1953), vol. 4, pp. 168–69.

4. Lincoln told his audience at the 1859 Wisconsin State Agricultural Society:

There is not, of necessity, any such thing as the free hired laborer being fixed to that condition for life. There is demonstration for saying this. Many independent men, in this assembly, doubtless a few years ago were hired laborers. . . .

The prudent, penniless beginner in the world, labors for wages awhile, saves a surplus with which to buy tools or land, for himself; then labors on his own account another while, and at length hires another new beginner to help him (Ibid., vol. 3, pp. 478–79).

5. See Nathan Rosenberg and L. E. Birdzell, Jr., *How the West Grew Rich: The Economic Transformation of the Industrial World* (New York: Basic Books, 1986).

6. G. K. Chesterton, *What's Wrong with the World*, ed. George J. Marlin et al. (San Francisco: St. Ignatius Press, 1987), pp. 65–66.

7. James Madison explained that property,

in its larger and juster meaning, . . . embraces every thing to which a man may attach a value and have a right; and *which leaves to every one else the like advantage*. . . .

A man has property in his opinions and the free communication of them.

He has a property of peculiar value in his religious opinions, and in the profession and practice dictated by them. . . .

He has an equal property in the free use of his faculties and free choice of the objects on which to employ them.

In a word, as a man is said to have a right to his property, he may be equally said to have a property in his rights (*The Papers of James Madison*, vol. 14, pp. 266–68 [emphasis in original]).

8. Novelist Mario Vargas Llosa, commenting on studies by Hernando de Soto, writes of the "informal" entrepreneurs of their native Peru:

In Lima alone, informal commerce (excluding manufacturing) provides work for some 445,000 people. Of the 331 markets in the city, 274 (83 percent) have been constructed by informals. With regard to transport, it is no exaggeration to say that the inhabitants of Lima can move around the city thanks to the informals since, according to the findings of the Institute [for Liberty and Democracy], 95 percent of the public transportation system of Lima belongs to them. "Peru's Silent Revolution: Despite Government Regulation, Entrepreneurs Are Rolling Back a Feudal Economic Order," *Crisis* (July–August 1987), p. 4.

CHAPTER 7: WEALTH AND VIRTUE

1. Kristol notes that

the terms 'prophetic' and 'rabbinic,' which come, of course, from the Jewish tradition, indicate the two poles within which the Jewish tradition operates. They are not two equal poles: The rabbinic is the stronger pole, always. In an Orthodox Hebrew school, the prophets are read only by those who are far advanced. The rest of the students read the first five books of the Bible, and no more. They learn the Law. The prophets are only for people who are advanced in their learning and not likely to be misled by prophetic fervor.

Orthodox Jews have never despised business; Christians have. The act of commerce, the existence of a commerical society, has always been a problem for Christians. Commerce has never been much of a problem for Jews. I have never met an Orthodox Jew who despised business—though I have met some Reformed Jews who are businessmen and despise business. . . .

Getting rich has never been regarded as being in any way sinful, degrading, or morally dubious within the Jewish religion, so long as such wealth is acquired legally and used responsibly. . . . It was generally assumed that the spirit of commerce is perfectly compatible with full religious faith and full religious practice. I think this is true in Islam as well, but it is not true in Christianity. The difference is that both Islam and Judaism are religions of the Law, and Christianity is a religion that has repealed the Law. This difference gives Christianity certain immense advantages over both Judaism and Islam in terms of spiritual energy; but in its application to the practical world, it creates enormous problems ("Christianity, Judaism, and Socialism," in *Reflections of a Neoconservative: Looking Back, Looking Ahead* [New York: Basic Books, Inc., 1983], p. 316–17).

For an account of economics within the framework of Jewish law and morality, see Meir Tamari, *With All Your Possessions: Jewish Ethics and Economic Life* (New York: Free Press, 1987).

2. John Adams wrote in 1809:

I will insist that the Hebrews have done more to civilize men than any other nation. If I were an atheist, and believed in blind eternal fate, I should still believe that fate had ordained the Jews to be the most essential instrument for civilizing the nations. If I were an atheist of the other sect, who believe or pretend to believe that all is ordered by chance, I should believe that chance had ordered the Jews to preserve and propagate to all mankind the doctrine of a supreme, intelligent, wise, almighty sovereign of the universe, which I believe to be the great essential principle of all morality, and consequently of all civilization (John Adams to F. A. Vanderkemp, February 16, 1809, in C. F. Adams, ed., *The Works of John Adams* [Boston: Little, Brown, 1854], vol. 9, pp. 609–10. Cited by Russell Kirk in *The Roots of American Order* [La Salle, Ill.: Open Court, 1974], p. 17).

3. "It is obvious," wrote Joseph Schumpeter,

that there would be no point in looking for 'economics' in the sacred writings themselves. The opinions on economic subjects that we might find—such as that believers should sell what they have and give it to the poor, or that they should lend without expecting anything (possibly not even repayment) from it—are ideal imperatives that form part of a general scheme of life and express this general scheme and nothing else, least of all scientific propositions (*History of Economic Analysis*, ed. Elizabeth Boody Schumpeter [New York: Oxford University Press, 1954], p. 71).

4. Michael Slattery, "The Catholic Origins of Capitalism," *Crisis*, vol. 6, no. 4 (April 1988), pp. 24–29. See also Leo Moulin, *L'Aventure Europeenne*

(Brussels: De Tempel, 1972), chap. 4–7; Alan MacFarlane, *The Culture of Capitalism* (New York: Basil Blackwell, 1987) (reviewed by Leonard P. Liggio in *Crisis*, vol. 6, no. 5 [May 1988], pp. 55–56.

5. See, for example, Adam Smith, *An Inquiry into the Nature and Causes of the Wealth of Nations*, 2 vols., ed. R. H. Campbell and A. S. Skinner (Indianapolis: Liberty Classics, 1976), I.xi.c, I.xi.1, and III.ii.

6. See Smith on the evils to which the "popular notion" that "wealth consists in money, or in gold and silver" can lead, in ibid. IV.i, pp. 429–51.

7. David Hume, "Of Commerce," in *Essays Moral, Political, and Literary*, edited and with a foreword, notes, and glossary by Eugene F. Miller, rev. ed. (Indianapolis: Liberty Classics, 1987), p. 258.

8. See "Of Avarice," ibid., pp. 569–73.

9. Jacques Leclercq remarks that in the premodern period "property was essentially landed property," that is, close to nature. But

> with the growth of technology, nature's contribution becomes restricted to supplying the raw materials for man's industry, which has discovered a large number of raw materials unknown to the ancients. More and more of the materials used by man for food and clothing are finished products, very different from natural products, such as fertilizers, tinned fruit and vegetables, and nylon fabrics. In other words, the materials employed by man in his daily life are coming to depend more and more on his labour: natural products are gradually displaced by man-made products. It is no longer felt that man merely enjoys the fruits of the earth bestowed on him by God: it seems as if man himself were the author or the creator, or at least the agent, of his own well-being (Jacques Leclercq, *Christianity and Money*, trans. Eric Earnshaw Smith [New York: Hawthorn Books, 1960], pp. 98–99).

10. See Norman Cohn, *The Pursuit of the Millennium*, rev. ed. (Oxford: Oxford University Press, 1970).

11. See Paul Johnson, "Has Capitalism a Future?" in *Will Capitalism Survive: A Challenge by Paul Johnson with Twelve Responses*, ed. Ernest W. Lefever (Washington, D.C.: Ethics and Public Policy Center, 1976), p. 5.

12. "In Montesquieu's analysis, it was the Christian Schoolmen, not the commerical practices they condemned, that deserved the label 'criminal.' In condemning something 'naturally permitted or necessary,' the doctrinaire and unworldly Scholastics set in train a series of misfortunes, most immediately for the Jews, more generally for Europe." See Ralph Lerner, *The Thinking Revolutionary: Principle and Practice in the New Republic* (Ithaca, N.Y.: Cornell University Press, 1987), p. 204, referring to Montesquieu, *The Spirit of the Laws*, Bk. 21, chap. 20.

13. See Colin McEvedy and Richard Jones, *Atlas of World Population History* (New York: Penguin Books, 1980), pp. 18, 342.

14. Geoffrey Bibby, *Four Thousand Years Ago: A World Panorama of Life in the Second Millennium B.C.* (New York: Alfred A. Knopf, 1962), chaps. 4, 13, and 14.

15. See Alan MacFarlane, *The Culture of Capitalism* (New York: Basil Blackwell Inc., 1987).

16. See Lester K. Little, *Religious Poverty and the Profit Economy in Medieval Europe* (Ithaca, N.Y.: Cornell University Press, 1978), part 4, "The Formation of an Urban Spirituality."

17. See Alejandro A. Chafuen, *Christians for Freedom: Late-Scholastic Economics* (San Francisco: Ignatius, 1986). In chap. 6, "Commerce, Merchants and Tradesmen," Chafuen notes that by the time of the Schoolmen, "commerce had long been held in low esteem by moralists of different countries, ages and backgrounds," and he suggests that the late Scholastics took two significant forward steps; first, they "found commercial activities to be morally indifferent," that is, not evil as thought previously, and they then "outlined the advantages of commerce" for society (p. 87).

18. Hume, "Of Commerce," p. 257.

19. John Locke, *Some Considerations of the Consequences of Lowering the Interest and Raising the Value of Money*, in *The Works of John Locke in Ten Volumes*, vol. 5 (London, 1823), p. 13.

20. "The chief difference," writes Hume, "between the domestic *œconomy* of the ancients and that of the moderns consists in the practice of slavery, which prevailed among the former, and which has been abolished for some centuries throughout the greater part of Europe." Hume adds: "The little humanity, commonly observed in persons, accustomed, from their infancy, to exercise so great authority over their fellow-creatures, and to trample upon human nature [is] sufficient alone to disgust us with that unbounded dominion." See Hume, "Of the Populousness of Ancient Nations," *Essays*, p. 383.

21. By demonstrating that moral distinctions are matters of sentiment, Hume had, at a single stroke, undermined the credibility of the entire casuistical tradition in the ancient and modern world. Hitherto, casuists had thought of virtuous conduct as the pursuit of universal goals. But no matter how attractive the prescriptions of these casuists might be . . . in a post-Humean world they seemed to be arbitrary and dependent on the whims of their authors rather than on a just appreciation of the principles of human nature (Nicholas Phillipson, "Adam Smith as Civic Moralist," in Istvan Hont and Michael Ignatieff, eds., *Wealth and Virtue: The Shaping of Political Economy in the Scottish Enlightenment* [Cambridge, Eng.: Cambridge University Press, 1983], p. 181).

See also, Adam Smith, "Of the Manner in Which Different Authors Have Treated the Practical Rules of Morality," in *Theory of Moral Sentiments*, with an introduction by E.G. West (Indianapolis: Liberty Classics, 1976), pp. 517–37.

22. "Higgling and bargaining" was a favorite phrase of Smith's, cited in *Wealth of Nations*, I.v.4–6; see also, II.iii.36 and III.iv.1–4.

23. Smith never discusses systematically when and how we acquire our moral education. He tells us that it is in the family that we first become aware that we are the objects of attention and learn that self-command is a useful habit to acquire in the search for approval, but he only deals in passing with the social experience we undergo thereafter. However, his language is suggestive; outside the family, the capacity for self-command and the rarer capacity for humanity is acquired in "societies," "associations," "companies," "clubs." It is the product of the "ordinary commerce of the world," in which

we seek "the wise security of friendship" by means of "conversation" which helps us to acquire ideas of "independence" and even
of "liberty" (Phillipson, "Adam Smith," *Wealth and Virtue*, pp. 187–
88).

24. Adam Smith, *Theory of Moral Sentiments*, I.i.5. (pp. 71–72).

25. Alasdair MacIntyre, *Whose Justice? Which Rationality?* (Notre Dame:
University of Notre Dame Press, 1988), pp. 164ff.

26. David Hume, *Lectures on Jurisprudence. Report of 1762–3.* Cited in Phillipson, "Adam Smith," p. 188.

27. Hume, "Of Commerce," *Essays*, pp. 260–61.

28. Ibid., p. 264.

29. Smith, *Wealth of Nations*, p. 418.

30. Ibid., III.iv.4, p. 412. See also, Hume's argument that the development
of commerce had the effect of drawing "authority and consideration to that
middling rank of men, who are the best and firmest basis of public liberty."
"Of Refinement in the Arts," *Essays*, p. 277.

31. In the coffee-houses, taverns and salons, men from different walks
of life confronted each other as friends and equals and learned that
conversation which was the instrument that forged the bonds of
friendship. By cultivating the arts of conversation and friendship
they would learn to value tolerance, detachment, moderation and a
respect for the value of consensus as a means of maintaining the
bonds of society (Phillipson, "Adam Smith," p. 189).

32. The more [the] refined arts advance, [writes Hume], the more
sociable men become. . . . They flock into cities; love to receive and
communicate knowledge; to show their wit or their breeding; their
taste in conversation or living, in clothes or furniture. Curiosity
allures the wise; vanity the foolish; and pleasure both. Particular
clubs and societies are everywhere formed. . . . Thus *industry,
knowledge,* and *humanity,* are linked together by an indissoluble chain
("Of Refinement in the Arts," *Essays*, p. 271).

Before the Seven Years' War . . . the most popular voluntary
institution [in Scotland] must have been the sort of club which was
modelled on Addison and Steele's Spectator Club. These clubs,
which met in the taverns and coffee-houses of countless provincial
towns and cities, were small, semi-formal institutions, drawing their
members from the ranks of the middling classes of these local
communities. Historically, the function of these clubs was to trans-
mit the culture of the metropolis to the provinces, adapting it to
local needs and ensuring that it would support and not threaten the
sense of identity of increasingly prosperous provincial communities
(Phillipson, "Adam Smith," *Wealth and Virtue*, p. 198).

33. Hume, "Of Commerce," *Essays*, p. 264.

34. Smith, *Wealth of Nations*, IV.iii.c, p. 493.

35. As far as Smith was concerned, the search for mutual sympathy
was a complex and demanding activity. . . . What is curious and
distinctive about Smith's theory is that he does not think that we
simply put ourselves in another man's shoes in order to see
whether, were we him, we would approve of what he was doing.

That would have introduced an element of egotism into the theory which he was particularly anxious to avoid. In his account we exercise our imaginative curiosity quite hard in order to achieve what we judge to be a genuinely critical detachment in our understanding of another man's behaviour (Phillipson, "Adam Smith," *Wealth and Virtue*, pp. 183–91).

36. Adam Smith and the Scottish social philosophers may be thought of as

practical moralists who had developed a formidable and complex casuistical armoury to instruct young men of middling rank in their duties as men and citizens of a modern commercial polity. Hutcheson, Smith, Ferguson, Reid and Stewart were professors of moral philosophy who saw their curricula as devices to teach their pupils to 'adorn your souls with every virtue, prepare yourselves for every honourable office in life and quench that manly and laudable thirst you should have after knowledge' " (Phillipson, ibid., p. 179).

For a discussion of Smith's pedagogical method of "presenting his readers (like the audience of fourteen- and fifteen-year-old students who had originally heard his lectures) with a large number of examples to remind them of the pleasure and pain which different types of social encounter could cause," see ibid., pp. 182–83.

37. See Aristotle's discussion of the happiness awaiting the person with a good nature who has been well educated, in *Nichomachean Ethics*, bk. 10, chaps. 6–9. On the education of children, in particular, on its difficulty, see bk. 10, chap. 9.

38. Albert O. Hirschman, *The Passions and the Interests: Political Arguments for Capitalism before Its Triumph* (Princeton: Princeton University Press, 1981).

39. Ibid., p. 32.

40. See Jacob Viner, "Power versus Plenty as Objectives of Foreign Policy in the Seventeenth and Eighteenth Centuries," *World Politics*, vol. 1 (1948), reprinted in D. C. Coleman, ed., *Revisions in Mercantilism* (London: Methuen, 1969), pp. 61–91.

41. *Wealth of Nations*, II.iii.28, p. 341–2.

42. Johann Christoph Friedrich von Schiller, *Wallenstein's Tod*, act I, sc. 6, line 37. Cited by Hirschman, *Passions and Interests*, p. 48.

43. "I have always considered him," wrote Adam Smith of his friend David Hume, "both in his lifetime and since his death, as approaching as nearly to the idea of a perfectly wise and virtuous man, as perhaps the nature of human frailty will permit." See this remarkable eulogy, in the form of a letter from Adam Smith to William Strahan, November 9, 1776, reprinted in Hume, *Essays*, pp. xliiv–ix.

44. Adam Smith was a "practical moralist who thought that his account of the principles of morals and social organization would be of use to responsibly-minded men of middling rank, living in a modern, commercial society" (Phillipson, "Adam Smith," *Wealth and Virtue*, p. 179).

45. Jules Feiffer, *Washington Post*, Aug. 27, 1989.

46. Michael H. Levin, "An Environmental Manifesto for Poland," *Wall Street Journal*, October 24, 1989.

47. See *Sollicitudo Rei Socialis*, no. 15.

48. See, for example, Hernando de Soto, *The Other Path: The Invisible Revolution in the Third World*, with a foreword by Mario Vargas Llosa (New York: Harper and Row, 1989).

CHAPTER 8: THE MORAL, CULTURAL, AND POLITICAL RESPONSIBILITIES
OF BUSINESS

1. Daniel Southerland, "China Calls for Boost in Private Enterprise: New Regulations Promote Production, Jobs," *Washington Post*, June 30, 1988.

2. See chap. 4, n. 8.

3. Mario Vargas Llosa in "Peru's Silent Revolution," *Crisis* (July–August 1987), summarizes a study prepared by Hernando de Soto's Institute for Liberty and Democracy:

> In Lima alone, informal commerce (excluding manufacturing) provides work for some 445,000 people. Of the 331 markets in the city, 274 (83 percent) have been constructed by informals. With regard to transport, it is no exaggeration to say that the inhabitants of Lima can move around the city thanks to the informals since, according to the findings of the Institute, 95 percent of the public transportation system of Lima belongs to them. Informals have invested more than $1 billion in the vehicles and maintenance facilities. In housing, the figures are equally impressive. Half of the population of Lima lives in homes constructed by informals. Between 1960 and 1984 the state built low-income housing at a cost of $173.6 million. In the same period, the informals built homes for the incredible sum of $8.2 billion (forty-seven times more than the state).

> 4. If one looks at the figures for the various countries of Latin America, one finds a wide range of percentages of state-generated GNP. It extends from about 35 to 40 percent (roughly equivalent to our own) in some of the lesser developed countries, Honduras or Guatemala, for example, to 50 or 55 percent in the Dominican Republic and to roughly 60 percent in Nicaragua. It further extends to about 65 or 70 percent in Mexico (with the nationalization of the banks and the various private concerns under the banks' domain) to about the same figure in Brazil, and to roughly 92 percent in Bolivia. . . . One could say that there is almost nothing left to nationalize in Bolivia (Howard J. Wiarda, "Economic and Political Statism in Latin America," in Michael Novak and Michael P. Jackson, eds., *Latin America: Dependency or Interdependence?* [Washington, D.C.: American Enterprise Institute, 1985], p. 6).

See also Mark Falcoff, "Political Systems and Economic Growth: The Case of Latin America," in Michael Novak, ed., *Liberation Theology and the Liberal Society* (Washington, D.C.: American Enterprise Institute, 1987).

5. Franz Cardinal Koenig comments on the use of "capitalism" in *Sollicitudo Rei Socialis*: " 'Capitalism' has many meanings. On the one hand, it can mean egoism, an excessive desire for money, exploitation. But it can also mean individual liberty, personal initiative, pluralism" (Tommaso Ricci, "And the Light Comes from the East," *30 Days*, June 1988, p. 53).

6. Hannah Arendt writes:

America had become the symbol of a society without poverty long before the modern age in its unique technological development had actually discovered the means to abolish that abject misery of sheer want which had always been held to be eternal. And only after this had happened and had become known to European mankind could the social question and the rebellion of the poor come to play a truly revolutionary role. The ancient cycle of sempiternal recurrences had been based upon an assumedly "natural" distinction of rich and poor; the factual existence of American society prior to the outbreak of the Revolution had broken this cycle once and for all (*On Revolution* [New York: Viking Press, 1965], pp. 15–16).

7. See Milovan Djilas, *The New Class* (New York: Praeger, 1957); and Bruno Rizzi, *The Bureaucratization of the World*, trans. Adam Westoby (New York: Free Press, 1985).

8. Quoted in George Gilder, "Trickle Up Economics: The Christian Basis for Capitalism," *Crisis* (July–August 1988).

9. Walter Lippmann, *The Good Society* (New York: Grosset & Dunlap, n.d.), pp. 193–94.

10. See Peter Berger, *The Capitalist Revolution* (New York: Basic Books, 1986).

CHAPTER 9: THE ECONOMIC PRECONDITIONS OF DEMOCRACY

1. "Latin American dictatorships consider themselves to be exceptional, provisional regimes. None of our dictators, not even the most brazen of them, has ever denied the historical legitimacy of democracy" (Octavio Paz, *One Earth, Four or Five Worlds: Reflections on Contemporary History*, trans. Helen R. Lane [New York: Harcourt Brace Jovanovich, 1983], p. 176); see also the chapter, "Latin America and Democracy," in ibid., pp. 158–88.

2. Hernando de Soto, *The Other Path: The Invisible Revolution in the Third World*, foreword by Mario Vargas Llosa, trans. June Abbott (New York: Harper & Row, 1989).

3. Addressing the U.S. Congress, Vaclav Havel said that since World War II we have learned

to see the world in bi-polar terms, as two enormous forces, one a defender of freedom, the other a source of nightmares. Europe became the point of friction between these two powers and thus it turned into a single enormous arsenal divided into two parts. In this process, one half of the arsenal became part of that nightmarish power, while the other—the free part—bordering on the ocean and having no wish to be driven into it, was compelled, together with you, to build a complicated security system, to which we probably owe the fact that we still exist ("Address of the President of the Czechoslovak Republic to a Joint Session of the United States Congress," Washington, D.C., February 21, 1990).

4. "The chief use of agricultural fairs," Abraham Lincoln said in his "Address to the Wisconsin State Agricultural Society" in Milwaukee,

is to aid in improving the great calling of agriculture, in all it's [sic] departments, and minute divisions—to make mutual exchange of agricultural discovery, information, and knowledge; so that, at the end, all may know every thing, which may have been known to but one, or to but a few, at the beginning. . . .

I know of nothing so pleasant to the mind, as the discovery of anything which is at once new and valuable—nothing which so lightens and sweetens toil, as the hopeful pursuit of such discovery. And how vast, and how varied a field is agriculture, for such discovery. The mind, already trained to thought, in the country school, or higher school, cannot fail to find there an exhaustless source of profitable enjoyment. Every blade of grass is a study; and to produce two, where there was but one, is both a profit and a pleasure. And not grass alone; but soils, seeds, and seasons— hedges, ditches, and fences, draining, droughts, and irrigation— plowing, hoeing, and harrowing—reaping, mowing, and thresh- ing—saving crops, pests of crops, diseases of crops, and what will prevent or cure them—implements, utensils, and machines, their relative merits, and how to improve them—hogs, horses, and cat- tle—sheep, goats, and poultry—trees, shrubs, fruits, plants, and flowers—the thousand things of which these are specimens—each a world of study within itself (Abraham Lincoln, *Speeches and Writings 1859–1865: Speeches, Letters and Miscellaneous Writings, Presidential Messages and Proclamations* [New York: Library of America, 1989], pp. 90–91, 99–100).

5. Guy Sorman, *Barefoot Capitalism*, English edition published in India, 1988.

Appendix: Thomas Aquinas, the First Whig

1. Friedrich A. Hayek, *The Constitution of Liberty* (Chicago: University of Chicago Press, 1978), p. 457, n. 4.

2. Thomas Aquinas, *An Essay on Christian Philosophy*, trans. Father Edward H. Flannery (New York: Philosophical Library, 1955), pp. 20, 21–22.

3. See Jacques Maritain, *Integral Humanism: Temporal and Spiritual Problems of a New Christendom*, trans. Joseph W. Evans (Notre Dame, Ind.: University of Notre Dame Press, 1973).

4. Acton quotes a text he attributes to Aquinas and appends his own comment, as follows:

"A king who is unfaithful to his duty forfeits his claim to obedience. It is not rebellion to depose him, for he is himself a rebel whom the nation has a right to put down. But it is better to abridge his power, that he may be unable to abuse it. For this purpose, the whole nation ought to have a share in governing itself; the Constitution ought to combine a limited and elective monarchy, with an aristoc- racy of merit, and such an admixture of democracy as shall admit all classes to office, by popular election. No government has a right to levy taxes beyond the limit determined by the people. All political authority is derived from popular suffrage, and all laws must be made by the people for their representatives. There is no security for us as long as we depend on the will of another man." This language, which contains the earliest exposition of the Whig theory of revolution, is taken from the works of St. Thomas Aquinas, of whom Lord Bacon says that he had the largest heart of the school divines. And it is worth while to observe that he wrote at the very moment when Simon de Montfort summoned the Commons; and that the politics of the Neapolitan friar are centuries in advance of the English statesman's ("The History of Freedom in Christianity," in Lord Acton, *Essays on Freedom and Power*, selected, and with a new introduction, by Gertrude Himmelfarb [New York: Meridian Books, 1955], p. 88).

5. Alexander Hamilton, James Madison, John Jay, *Federalist 10*, *The Federalist*, with an introduction, table of contents, and index of ideas by Clinton Rossiter (New York: New American Library of World Literature, 1961), p. 81; see also the reference to "Utopian speculations," *Federalist 6*.

6. See Hayek's essay, "Why I Am Not a Conservative," in *The Constitution of Liberty*, pp. 397–411.

7. "With respect to our rights, and the acts of the British government contravening those rights," Jefferson writes about the Declaration of Independence, "there was but one opinion on this side of the water. All American Whigs thought alike on these subjects" (Letter to Henry Lee, May 8, 1825, in *The Life and Selected Writings of Thomas Jefferson*, ed. by Adrienne Koch and William Peden [New York: Modern Library, 1972], p. 719). See also, Hayek, *The Constitution of Liberty*, p. 409.

8. *Federalist 14*. See also Hamilton's remark that "experience [is] the least fallible guide of human opinions," *Federalist 6*.

9. Thomas Gilby quoted in John Courtney Murray, *We Hold These Truths: Catholic Reflections on the American Proposition* (New York: Sheed and Ward, 1960), p. 6.

10. *Saint Thomas Aquinas: Philosophic Texts*, selected and translated by Thomas Gilby (New York: Oxford University Press, 1960), p. 370 (*Commentary*, *I Politics*, lect. I), and p. 356 (III *Contra Gentiles*, III–16). On the need for collaboration among reasonable creatures, Saint Thomas writes that

Man . . . has a natural knowledge of the things which are essential for his life only in a general fashion, inasmuch as he is able to attain knowledge of the particular things necessary for human life by reasoning from natural principles. But it is not possible for one man to arrive at a knowledge of all these things by his own individual reason. It is therefore necessary for man to live in a multitude so that each one may assist his fellows, and different men may be occupied in seeking, by their reason, to make different discoveries— one, for example, in medicine, one in this and another in that (Saint Thomas Aquinas, *On Kingship*, trans. Gerald B. Phelan, revised with an introduction and notes by I. Th. Eschmann, O.P. [Toronto: Pontifical Institute of Medieval Studies, 1949], p. 5).

11. The point can be illustrated by the place Saint Thomas gives to reason in his account of law. Law is not primarily compulsion because it

is something pertaining to reason. Though reason itself receives its impulse from the will, for the reason issues its commands about means because the end is willed, nevertheless, the willing of what is commanded must be regulated by the reason to be endowed with the strength of law: this reasonableness must be read into the dictum that the will of the prince has the force of law; otherwise would it be lawlessness rather than law (See *Philosophic Texts*, p. 354 [*Summa Theologica*, 1a-2ae.xc.I,c. and ad 3]).

12. Thomas sums up his position thus: "Considered in themselves as motions of the sensitive and non-rational appetite, passions are neither right nor wrong, for morality depends on the reason. They are covered by morality in so far as they are subject to the sway of reason and will" (See *Philosophic Texts*, p. 296 [*Summa Theologica*, Ia-2ae.xxiv.I]).

13. "By nature," Aquinas writes, "all men are equal in liberty, but not in other endowments. One man is not subordinate to another as though he were a utility." Similarly, "by sinning, a man falls back from the level of reason, and to that extent loses the dignity of a human person free within and existing in his own right. He falls into the slavish condition of the beasts *Philosophical Texts*, p. 385, 389 (*Commentary, II Sentences*, XLIV. i.3, ad 1. and *Summa Theologica*, 2a-2ae. lxiv.2, ad 3):

> The end which befits a multitude of free men is different from that which befits a multitude of slaves, for the free man is one who exists for his own sake, while the slave, as such, exists for the sake of another. If, therefore, a multitude of free men is ordered by the ruler toward the common good of the multitude, that rulership will be right and just, as is suitable to free men (*On Kingship*, p. 177).

14. *Philosophical Texts*, pp. 355–56 (*Contra Gentiles*, III–16).

15. On the consensual basis of political rule, see Saint Thomas's remark that "the government of tyrants . . . cannot last long because it is hateful to the multitude, and what is against the wishes of the multitude cannot be long preserved" (*On Kingship*, p. 194).

16. Saint Thomas writes: "If to provide itself with a king belongs to the right of a given multitude, it is not unjust that the king be deposed or have his power restricted by that same multitude if, becoming a tyrant, he abuses the royal power" (ibid., p. 27).

17. "Virtue," writes Saint Thomas, "is a good habit"; and "Virtue in the emotional appetites is their habitual conformity with reason" (*Philosophical Texts*, p. 301, 308 [*Summa Theologica*, Ia-2ae. 1v. 3, and ibid., Ia-2ae. 1vi. 4]).

18. *Philosophic Texts*, p. 390 (III *Contra Gentiles*, 80).

19. Ibid., p. 392 (*Summa Theologica*, Ia. xxix. 2).

20. Ibid., p. 356 7 (III *Contra Gentiles*, III–16).

21. Those who are kept down by fear will rise against their rulers if the opportunity ever occurs when they can hope to do it with impunity, and they will rebel against their rulers all the more furiously the more they have been kept in subjection against their will by fear alone, just as water confined under pressure flows with greater impetus when it finds an outlet. . . . Therefore the government of a tyrant cannot be of long duration (*On Kingship*, p. 47).

22. Ibid., p. 382 (*Summa Theologica*, Ia-2ae. cv. I).

23. See Alasdair MacIntyre, *After Virtue* (Notre Dame: University of Notre Dame Press, 1981).

24. See William J. Abraham "Oh God, Poor God: The State of Contemporary Theology," *American Scholar* (Autumn 1989), pp. 557–63. Glenn Tinder has suggested a way to heal this rift in our public life in "Can We Be Good without God?" *Atlantic Monthly*, vol. 264, no. 6 (December 1989), pp. 69–85.

25. *Commentary, I Politics*, lect. I.

26. Ibid.

27. See James Q. Wilson, "The Rediscovery of Character," *Public Interest*, vol. 81 (Fall 1985).

28. See MacIntyre, *After Virtue;* Stanley Hauerwas, *Vision and Virtue* (South Bend, Ind.: Fides/Claretian, 1974); and *A Community of Character: Toward a Constructive Christian Social Ethic* (Notre Dame: University of Notre Dame Press, 1981); and James M. Gustafson, *Christ and the Moral Life* (New York: Harper and Row, 1968).

29. See Joel Schwartz, "The Rights of Nature and the Death of God," *Public Interest*, no. 97 (Fall 1989), pp. 3–14.

30. Thomas Gilby, *The Political Thought of Thomas Aquinas* (Chicago: University of Chicago Press, 1958), p. 102.

31. *Philosophical Texts*, p. 392 (*Summa Theologica*, Ia.xxix.2).

32. Jacques Maritain, *The Person and the Common Good* (Notre Dame: University of Notre Dame Press, 1972), p. 20.

Index

voluntary association, 20–23
as Whig principles, 5, 7, 9, 14, 25
Peru, 92, 102
Pesch, Heinrich, 27, 130 n.9
Philippines, 98
Philosophy, 110–11
Pico della Mirandola, Giovanni, 73
Pieper, Josef, 110
Pilgrims, 15
Plato, 16, 108, 114
Poland, 19, 83, 85–86, 98, 122
Political economy
Latin America, 4, 57–59, 92, 102
liberating form of, 49, 51–52
meaning, 12–13
See also Enterprise
Political liberty, 14, 46, 90, 97–98, 102, 106
Political regimes
Aquinas's theses, 114–19
Whig institutions, 120–22
See also Specific regimes
Political science, 120–22
Politics (Aristotle), 26, 109
Population figures, 71, 89
Portugal, 98
Positive law, 116
Post-Communist society, 8
Poverty, 51
amelioration. *See* Enterprise
immorality of, 26
premodern society characterized, 74–76
Socialist view, 59
Power, 11
Practical wisdom, 3, 7, 10, 31, 117
Precapitalist economy, 58, 71, 85
characteristics, 4, 53, 92, 104
wealth creation in, 97
Principles of Political Economy (Mill), 26
Privatization, 105
Progress, 89, 95
Whig value, 3, 121–22
Progressive thought, 2, 3, 10, 112
Proletariat class, 94
Property ownership, 49, 52–55, 105, 121
Providence, 10
Prudence, 10
Public interest, 42
Public Philosophy, The (Lippmann), 8

Radical thought, 2
Ratzinger, Josef, Cardinal, 9
Rawls, John, 74
Reactionary thought, 2
Reagan, Ronald, 40, 99
Reason, 3, 31, 115, 117, 119
Reasoned discourse, 19, 114–15

Reflection and choice, 26, 103, 115–17
Reflections on America (Maritain), 23
Reid, Thomas, 72, 139 n.36
Religious liberty. *See* Morality
Religious tradition. *See* Jewish and Christian ethos
Republican government, 30
Rerum Novarum (Leo XIII), 43
Richard III (king of England), 108
Rightful liberty. *See* Ordered liberty
Roepke, Wilhelm, 9
Rome, 111
Rousseau, Jean-Jacques, 120

Savings, 31–32
Schiller, Johann C. F. von, 81
Scholastics (Schoolmen), 71, 72–73, 136 n.17
Schumpeter, Joseph, 135 n.3
Scottish Enlightenment, 6, 63, 72, 74–78, 85, 87–88, 139 n.36
Seal of the United States, 40, 43–44
Self-interest, 13, 38–39, 41–43, 81–82, 97
Sentiment, 78–83, 115
Shakespeare, William, 108
Simon, Yves R., 3, 9, 110
Sin, 3, 11, 39
Singapore, 46, 49, 51, 98
Sistine Chapel frescoes, 108
Slavery, 71–73
Smith, Adam, 68, 72, 113
moral vision, 73–83, 85
political economy, 12, 26–28, 72
Soares, Mario, 98
Social democracy, 57, 108
Socialism, 27
deficiencies and decline, 32, 55, 59, 85–86, 98
tenets, 3, 89
Social market economy, 106
Social vision
commercial republic, 13–14
Jewish and Christian ethos, 46–47, 66–68, 85–88
necessary architecture, 7, 14, 27, 89–99, 105–6
Whig perspective, 9–11, 24
Solidarity, 8, 9, 20
Sollicitudo Rei Socialis (John Paul II), 9, 28, 44
Sorman, Guy, 104
South Korea, 46, 49, 51, 59–60, 98
Soviet Union, 22, 83, 85, 86, 91, 93, 95
Spain, 98
Spirit of Democratic Capitalism, The (Novak), 4
Spiritualizers, 66

About the Author

MICHAEL NOVAK holds the George Frederick Jewett Chair in Religion and Public Policy at the American Enterprise Institute in Washington, D.C., where he also serves as director of social and political studies. In 1986, with the rank of ambassador, he headed the U.S. Delegation to the Experts' Meeting on Human Contacts at the Conference on Security and Cooperation in Europe, held in Bern, Switzerland. In 1981 and 1982 he led the U.S. Delegation to the United Nations Human Rights Commission in Geneva. Mr. Novak has taught at Harvard, Stanford, Syracuse, and Notre Dame.

The author of numerous monographs, articles, and reviews, he has written over twenty influential books in philosophy, theology, political economy, and culture. Among the best known are *The Spirit of Democratic Capitalism; Will it Liberate? Questions about Liberation Theology; Freedom with Justice: Catholic Social Thought and Liberal Institutions;* and *Free Persons and the Common Good.* Mr. Novak is also the founder and publisher of *Crisis,* a lay Catholic journal, and a columnist for *Forbes Magazine.*

A NOTE ON THE BOOK

*This book was edited by Dana Lane of the
publications staff of the American Enterprise Institute.
The index was prepared by Patricia Ruggiero.
The text was set in Palatino, a typeface designed by
the twentieth-century Swiss designer Hermann Zapf.
Coghill Composition Company, of Richmond, Virginia,
set the type, and Edwards Brothers Incorporated,
of Ann Arbor, Michigan, printed and bound the book,
using permanent acid-free paper.*

The AEI PRESS is the publisher for the American Enterprise Institute for
Public Policy Research, 1150 17th Street, N.W., Washington, D.C. 20036:
Christopher C. DeMuth, publisher; *Edward Styles,* director; *Dana Lane,* editor;
Ann Petty, editor; *Cheryl Weissman,* editor; *Susan Moran,* editorial assistant
(rights and permissions). Books published by the AEI PRESS are distributed
by arrangement with the University Press of America, 4720 Boston Way,
Lanham, Md. 20706.

www.ingramcontent.com/pod-product-compliance
Lightning Source LLC
Jackson TN
JSHW011938131224
75386JS00041B/1442